CLEAN
LIKE A MAN

CLEAN
LIKE A MAN

HOUSEKEEPING FOR MEN
{ AND THE WOMEN WHO LOVE THEM }

TOM M^cNULTY

Three Rivers Press
New York

Published by Three Rivers Press, New York,
New York. Member of the Crown Publishing Group,
a division of Random House, Inc.
www.crownpublishing.com

THREE RIVERS PRESS and the tugboat design are registered
trademarks of Random House, Inc.

Printed in the United States of America

Design by Caitlin Daniels Israel
Illustrations by Jim Specht

Library of Congress Cataloging-in-Publication Data
McNulty, Tom.
Clean like a man: housekeeping for men (and the women
who love them) / Tom McNulty.
1. House cleaning.   I. Title.
TX324.M39   2004
648'.5—dc22   2003014673

ISBN 1-4000-4975-X

10 9 8 7 6 5 4 3 2 1

FIRST EDITION

This book is lovingly dedicated to Phil and Mary Ann McNulty,
who taught me how to live cleanly and well.

Contents

Introduction

When I was ten or so, my mother said I had to start making my bed before heading off to school. So every morning, still lying there, I'd pull the sheet this way, the blanket that way, then slide easily out from underneath the whole thing, and presto: Just a few tucks and pillow fluffings later, the bed was made. Not perfect, mind you . . . but *good enough.*

The point is, it was the *manly* thing to do: complete a chore with a minimum of time and effort, then get on with our lives.

I believe most men are programmed this way, both by genetics and through our culture. While we appreciate a clean, tidy space as much as anyone, we don't *enjoy* dusting, vacuuming, and picking up after ourselves. But who'll do this stuff if we don't? Either an expensive cleaning service or an angry woman, that's who.

That's why there's *Clean Like a Man,* a book that delivers housekeeping how-to from a guy's point of view. Its premise: Our problem with cleaning isn't a matter of laziness or indifference; it's ignorance. *We just don't know how.* We have no idea where to start, what tools to use, or how to do it right. We are confused. And even if we *try* to clean the house, our ineptitude makes it frustrating, a waste of time, and hugely negative reinforcement.

No more! *Clean Like a Man* is filled with manly advice, tips, and techniques for cleaning and organizing: how to get motivated to tackle housework, get it all done faster, and then keep your place looking its best with the *least* amount of effort. Maybe not perfect, but certainly good enough for a guy.

What's more, *Clean Like a Man* focuses only on housekeeping tasks that matter to men. It will not discuss feng shui, arts and crafts, recipes, interior decorating, origami, centerpieces, or anything else that smacks of Martha Stewart. It *will* tell you how to treat the stains men get on carpets and clothing, tidy up in a flash when guests are due, clean the bathroom in minutes, make sure your bedroom appeals to women rather than appalls them, turn your vacuum cleaner into a high-performance dusting machine, get instant advice when you're in a jam, and much more. You'll even find out when it's time to give up and "go pro": locate and select a cleaning service.

All this is real *Clean Like a Man* stuff, and it's as easy as mastering the basic housecleaning tools and techniques—then discovering the many tips, tricks, secrets, and shortcuts that can save you hours of work, buckets of money, and worlds of hurt. Some of it is such good information that lots of women don't even know about it yet.

Maybe most important, *Clean Like a Man* is written in a just-the-facts style that minimizes words and maximizes useful information, so you can zero in on what you need to know fast.

After all, your time is valuable. And there's probably a big game on ESPN right now.

The Truth About Housekeeping

There are men who actually clean for a living: janitors—the Green Berets of male cleaning. They are elite, battle-hardened professionals whose usual combat zones are schools, hospitals, office buildings . . . much larger spaces than most of us guys will ever encounter. But as daunting as their tasks may be, janitors are never intimidated. These men fear nothing, and neither should you. Because the guidelines janitors follow to do their jobs are the same ones every man can use when tidying up his house. Plus, most of them are as easy as a one-inch putt.

You don't have to possess a superhuman intellect to clean the house. Except for Matt Damon's character in *Good Will Hunting*, few if any janitors can solve MIT-level math problems, and you don't need to memorize hundreds of different stain-removal formulas to succeed. Housekeeping is a lot simpler than that.

All a man needs to clean the house is opposable thumbs, a few supplies, and a little know-how and motivation. You already have the thumbs. *Clean Like a Man* will give you the rest.

You'll learn how to select and use the best housecleaning tools and supplies, then get cleaning done faster, easier, and cheaper than you ever imagined. So let's start with the simple fact that's about to change your life forever. . . .

A Little Know-How Is a *Huge* Advantage

While women spent the nineties empowering themselves, men were going to encounter groups to learn how to be politically correct and get in touch with our feelings. But nobody taught us how to get in touch with a vacuum cleaner.

Our basic problem with housekeeping isn't apathy, it's lack of knowledge. Most of us simply don't know how to do it right—and *that's* what makes it seem like such an ordeal. If you're using crappy equipment or chimplike methods, you'll just make small jobs big and easy ones difficult, which really ruins the fun.

What's in It for You?

Housekeeping certainly doesn't provide the same guy-thing gratification as Humvees, NFC wild-card games, or *Baywatch* reruns. But it does have some pretty good upsides. A few examples:

POSITIVE OUTLOOK

Living in a clean, organized home has a positive effect on both body and soul. It creates a sense of serenity and order. You feel good about yourself and the world, you're more productive, and you're happier.

BETTER HEALTH

Good housekeeping is good for you. Mold, bacteria, mildew, and other nasty microorganisms thrive in a dirty environment and can cause or aggravate many ailments, from colds to allergies.

LESS STRESS

An orderly house inspires an orderly, low-hassle life. Psychological stress has been shown to trigger all sorts of physical problems, from high blood pressure and insomnia to heart disease and cancer. Why not sidestep all of this if you can?

MORE "AMORE"

Your wife or girlfriend will really love you for being so considerate and keeping the place nice, which is good for the kind of domestic bliss that money just can't buy.

IT'S FREE

You'll save a lot of money cleaning your own house. It's not just the several hundred bucks you could easily spend on a cleaning service every month, either. Dirt wears things out more quickly: wood floors, carpets, appliances, clothing, upholstery, countertops. Clean stuff lasts longer.

YOU CAN USE MACHINES

This is hugely important in the *Clean Like a Man* world. The main housecleaning machine, the vacuum cleaner, has evolved into a high-performance, space-age piece of equipment. While they're not as much fun to operate as chain saws or backhoes, today's best vacuums are powerful, high-tech units with ingenious attachments that cut the most dreaded tasks down to size.

Work Smarter, Not Harder

Some things in this life are inevitable: Dirt and dust rank right up there with death and taxes. After all, the whole planet is one big ball of soil. Some of it is bound to get into your house. Unless you hire a cleaning service to come in every couple of weeks, or you're married to some sort of June Cleaver, or you simply don't care about an unkempt environment, you must accept the fact that you'll have to clean your own house. The good news is that housecleaning can be a snap, if you work smarter. And after you read *Clean Like a Man*, you *will* be working smarter.

part one

CHALK TALK

{Housekeeping Basics}

For most guys, the first few chapters of *Clean Like a Man* will be Housekeeping 101—a crash course for all men who never took a home economics class, scraped mildew from shower tile, sewed on a button, or ever cared less about any of it. In other words, 99 percent of us.

THE MEN COMMANDMENTS

Housecleaning Rules of Thumb

Professional housecleaners accomplish a lot in very little time because they follow some basic rules. These are good, commonsense fundamentals that both men and women should adhere to. But men have their own unique challenges. So *Clean Like a Man* took the basics and retooled them to be as guy-friendly as possible. Result: the Men Commandments (ironically, there are ten of them). They provide essential know-how in the manly quest to streamline housekeeping, and they're so simple that you should take to them like a cop to a doughnut.

1. Get Started

This is always the toughest part of housekeeping for men, but it's the most important. Why don't we start? Because we don't know *where* to start! There seems to be so much to do that you don't know what to do first. Cleaning the house has become an eight-hundred-pound gorilla. Or, more aptly, an intimidating mountain of mess (see "The K2 Syndrome" on page 19).

The best way to start is to decide the one room you want to

work on: the kitchen, for example. Don't think about anything else. Go in there and take a minute to look around. What's bugging you most? Crumbs on the counter? Dishes in the sink? Decomposing food in the fridge? Dirty windows? Clutter? All the crap held by magnets on the refrigerator door? Start with the job that will have the biggest impact when completed. Better yet, *write down* a list of to-dos for that room, put them in order of priority, and handle them . . . *one at a time.*

2. Pick Up the Place First

Shoes and socks, scattered newspapers, plates, coffee mugs, knives and forks, half-read Tolstoy novels . . . all the stuff that's strewn about the room serves only to get in your way and distract you from the real job at hand: cleaning. You can't get at dirt and dust on the carpets or counters if it's covered up with junk. So clear the decks.

Make a clockwise sweep of the room, toss everything into a big box, a closet, or even into another room, and then you're ready for some serious cleaning. Just picking up by itself is a huge improvement.

MANDATORY ADVICE
Say No to Knickknacks

There's nothing more maddening than to be dusting and get to a tabletop that's filled with dozens of junky little figurines, bric-a-brac, curios, ornaments, tchotchkes, delft pieces, or someone's prized collection of whatnots. It's a definite momentum-buster. So if you're going to make a good run at housecleaning, I recommend getting this stuff out of your life. Forever.

3. Divide and Conquer

Contemplating the *entire* job ahead will only discourage you. Break each chore down into room-by-room "quadrants." Focus on one room at a time. Or chop it into even smaller pieces: one swath of carpet to vacuum, one shelf to dust. Things seem more manageable. Your focus sharpens, you work more efficiently, and being 100 percent done with *something* gives you a feeling of accomplishment.

4. Carry Your Supplies with You

Any project takes longer and is more frustrating when you continually have to stop your work and go look for a tool. Same with housekeeping. So tote basic cleaning supplies—all-purpose sprays, carpet spot treatment, a few sponges and cloths, a whisk broom and dustpan—in whatever kind of carryall works best for you.

If you have a bigger arsenal of gear, you might want to load it onto some sort of serving cart on wheels. If you have less stuff or are on a more limited mission, go with a tool belt that has your most important equipment and supplies in the pockets.

Having all your goods at your fingertips saves constant trips from one room to another—or worse, from floor to floor—to fetch items. What's more, you never have to stop your work and ruin your momentum to hunt down something you need.

5. Deploy Supplies Where You Use Them

Place your most-used cleaning tools and supplies in strategic spots around the house to allow instant, easy access. For example, under your bathroom sink should be a sponge, a toilet brush, and a container of cleanser for the john; a spray bottle of Windex for the mirror, the sink, and the fixtures (plus a cotton rag and paper towels); Lysol and Tilex to spray into the shower or the tub and onto the curtain and the tiles to battle mildew; and a Swiffer or ReadyMop to get dust and stray hairs off tile or linoleum in a flash. You can stash a similar cache under the kitchen sink, and add a small hand vacuum and/or a whisk broom–dustpan combo for dry spills, and paper towels to clean up small wet spills.

This kind of planning will save you plenty of running around to find the appropriate tools and supplies when you need 'em.

6. Start High, Finish Low

Gravity—it's the law! Clean from the top down, ceiling to floor. The reason is simple: When you stir up dust and dirt, they float earthward. So . . .

* Begin by cleaning high: removing cobwebs from ceiling corners, dusting the tops of cabinets, ledges above windows and doors, shelves, ceiling fans, light fixtures.
* Move next to eye level to dust and clean picture frames, lamp shades, TVs, and bookcases.
* Finish low with chairs and sofas, tables, and, last but not least, floors.

7. Get the Right Stuff

Using the best cleaning supplies (both tools and products) makes housekeeping faster, easier, and less aggravating. Spend a few cents more to purchase brand names you've heard of. They're famous for a reason, and they're specifically formulated for specialized jobs. You can find almost everything you'll require at your local hardware store, home center, discount store, drugstore, or supermarket. If you go to a janitorial-supply store, trust the expert to steer you in the right direction. Cutting corners means you'll be using tools and supplies that just aren't as good as they could be, which will make your job harder than it has to be.

8. Give Cleaning Solutions Time to Work

After you've sprayed a surface with the appropriate solution, let it sit awhile before you scrub. For example, wet down the mineral deposits in the shower with Lime-A-Way and then go clean something else for a few minutes. When you come back, you won't have to scrub as hard to get the walls clean. And you MANaged your time well by getting something else done in the interim.

9. Finish What You Start

Don't move on until whatever you're working on—the room, the carpet, the coffee table, *whatever*—is completely done. Then you'll have at least one thing 100 percent accomplished, instead of several things only partially finished.

10. Don't Clean Too Much

Even housekeeping experts say that cleaning too much or too often isn't good: Too-frequent vacuumings and shampooings wear out carpeting fibers faster, scrubbing rubs away wall paint, and so on. So sweep that guilt under a rug . . . you're doing fine!

THE K2 SYNDROME: Killer of Manly Motivation

Imagine standing at the foot of K2, the world's second tallest mountain, and all you see between yourself and the summit is ten miles—mostly up—of neck-deep snow, subzero temperatures, towering glaciers, bottomless crevasses, sheer cliffs, thin air, killer storms, and exhausting physical exertion. That's enough to make even your Sherpas head back to the hotel.

The K2 Syndrome is a common state of mind among men who try to clean. You're so overwhelmed and intimidated by the immensity of your mission that you give up before you even start and wind up doing nothing.

There's only one way to conquer this hopeless feeling: just take one MANageable step at a time. Each step is an accomplishment that moves you closer to your objective.

With housekeeping, it's easy to beat the K2 Syndrome by narrowing your focus to a single room, or one side of a room, or just one tabletop. Clean the house like you'd climb a mountain: one step at a time.

The Men Commandments—Extra Points

Here's an extra batch of tips and tricks specially geared to guys. They're not as top-tier as the first ten but they're great ways to save time and trouble.

DON'T BE OVERLY FUSSY

We call this "being too Felix," in honor of Felix Unger, the guy in *The Odd Couple* who was compulsively clean and annoyingly neat. You probably won't have too much trouble following this rule. It's important to have reasonable standards of cleanliness, but if you're overly persnickety, you'll never be satisfied. Or it will take you a whole lot longer to get to the point at which you're happy.

A manly rule of thumb is: If you can't see it, don't clean it. Dusting the tops of cupboards and overhead fan blades, for example, are tasks that have "once a year" written all over them. Has someone ever climbed up there to look for dust? Or gotten down on all fours to check under the sofa? If it *looks* done, consider it done for now. You'll have to clean it eventually. But nothing in your house really has to be *hyper*clean—you're not living in an operating room, after all.

SPRITZ, DON'T SPLASH

Mixing bucketfuls of cleaning solution is a pain, as is continually dipping in a sponge, wringing it, cleaning with it, rinsing it, and repeating. Instead, purchase as many of your cleaning products as possible in spray containers, or mix cleaning solutions in spray bottles. Then *spritz* the appropriate solution onto surfaces, let it work, and sponge it up or wipe it clean with a rag. Tote along a small pail of water only to rinse out your sponge.

Try cleaning a few countertops both ways and you'll see that the "spray and wash" (what a great name for a product!) method is much easier than the "slosh and wash" approach.

GO THOREAU

I recently moved from a big house to a smaller one, and I have yet to unpack about half my belongings. I don't miss any of it, which tells me I don't need it. So I see the Goodwill truck and a charitable tax deduction in the future. So can you!

* If you own less stuff, you'll have less stuff to clean.
* The uncluttered look is very soothing. Almost all of your cleaning becomes a matter of a little light dusting and vacuuming.

Look at your own collection: old clothes you haven't worn in a year, esoteric tools you haven't used in who knows how long, files of ancient documents. If you can be unsentimental enough to give most of it away, do it. You'll never regret it.

SPOT-CLEAN WHENEVER POSSIBLE

One fingerprint on the fridge is no reason to clean the entire fridge. If there's a small spot on the carpet, it doesn't mean you have to call a carpet-cleaning service. Do you head for the dentist's office when you have a poppy seed in your teeth? No. Do as little as you can. It's the *Clean Like a Man* credo.

USE YOUR VACUUM AS MUCH AS YOU CAN

Invest in a high-quality machine. It will make your work much quicker and easier, while a crappy one will do just the opposite. The vacuum cleaner—especially a newer one with all the bells and whistles—is an invention that ranks right up there with the wheel and the printing press. It's so important that *Clean Like a Man* devotes a good amount of space in the next chapter to discussing its merits, most desirable features, most effective vacuuming techniques, and how to get the best value when you buy one.

SET A TIME LIMIT AND THEN RUSH, RUSH, RUSH ...

This is one of the most psychologically valuable things you can do when cleaning. Racing the clock takes the "deer in the headlights" factor out of large housecleaning jobs that can be intimidating. So tell yourself, "I'll clean like crazy for thirty minutes, but that's it." Turn yourself into a perpetual-motion machine, and you'll be surprised at how much you can get done in that half-hour of focused, frenzied effort. When time is up, you can certainly stop and bask in your accomplishment, but you'll often keep going. It's the momentum. It's like setting off to run a marathon versus starting a one-mile jog: The marathon will take a pretty good part of your day, but you'll be done with the mile in about eight minutes.

It's a toss-up as to what will be more effective for you: setting a time limit and seeing how far you can get, or setting a goal of completing, say, one room in fifteen minutes. Either way is helpful. And Chapter 7 will tell you how to squeeze the most out of your housekeeping time by treating it as an "event" rather than a torturous ordeal.

... BUT DON'T RUSH THE WRONG THINGS

It seems funny to suggest taking your time right after I tell you to hurry. But this harkens back to the "let the chemicals do the work" rule and it's worth repeating: If you spray a cleaning solution on a surface, let it do its work awhile. This might involve using Formula 409 to dissolve crud on a greasy countertop (a couple of minutes), spraying Resolve on a carpet stain (ten minutes), or

HOME **MAN**AGEMENT TIP
The More You Do It, the Easier It Gets

Once a place is clean and orderly, it's fairly simple to maintain it. Keeping your house clean becomes an ongoing, low-maintenance process requiring just a few minutes a day. Putting dishes in the dishwasher, rather than piling them in the sink; having a place to store old newspapers for recycling, instead of leaving them on the coffee table; squeegeeing the shower tiles after every use, Windexing the bathroom mirror, wiping off kitchen counters, making the bed . . . it's all a matter of handling small jobs that together have a big impact.

soaking a barbecue grill grate in soapy water (overnight). It turns the dirt, grease, stain, or gunk into something you can easily wipe away. It will take a little more time but a lot less elbow grease when you let the chemicals do most of the dirty work.

CLEAN AS YOU GO

Make it a habit to pick up after yourself to keep things uncluttered; take care of small things now to avoid big chores later. If you clean regularly, the job won't build up to a monumental task.

DON'T WASH CLOTHES AFTER EVERY WEARING

Unless you don't bathe regularly, a shirt or a pair of jeans or slacks is probably perfectly wearable two or three times before it needs washing. Overlaundering clothes wears them out faster. And if you toss something in the wash to avoid folding, hanging, or storing it—a typically male motive—well, you'll have to fold it and put it away when it comes out of the dryer, won't you?

BUT *DO* WASH DISHES AFTER EVERY MEAL

It's tempting to let them sit in the sink, but this allows food to harden and bacteria to establish a beachhead there. Even worse is to let them soak: Bacteria still breeds, you get grease slicks on the water surface, it looks awful, and eventually it smells, too. Force yourself to wash dishes right away, or at least rinse them off and put them in the dishwasher.

CLEAN AND DISINFECT THE KITCHEN A LOT

You may not be able to see bacteria, but they're there. In the sink, on counters, on cutting boards, just about everywhere. But they don't belong in the kitchen. It's very important to keep food-preparation surfaces as sanitary as possible. So use Lysol or another disinfecting cleaner both before and after you do your meal prep.

MULTITASK

There are scores of multitasking opportunities that will become self-evident to you as you clean. While you don't have to be cleaning house all the time, you might as well take care of as much

HOME **MAN**AGEMENT TIP
Make Tidiness a Habit

Eliminating most of your careless, mess-producing practices can become second nature very easily. It's a matter of dealing with minor, momentary inconveniences that can escalate into huge eyesores and lengthy cleanups. For example:

> Toss all your laundry-bound clothes into a strategically placed hamper instead of leaving them where they happen to fall.
>
> Gather up all scattered newspapers and put them into a recycling container.
>
> Keep tabletops free of dishware, glasses, and delft knickknacks.
>
> Vacuum carpets weekly, especially those in high-traffic areas.
>
> Consolidate whenever possible. If there are ten books or magazines lying about, put them into a single stack. Then storing the stack out of view is even better.
>
> After preparing a meal, rinse all the pans and the dishes and place them into the dishwasher. (If you don't have a dishwasher, *Clean Like a Man*'s advice is to either get one or move to a place that has one.)
>
> After showering, wipe water droplets off the tile and the glass doors with a towel or a squeegee to avoid water spots and mineral deposits.
>
> If you don't have a dog, sponge up morsels of food you drop *as you drop them!* There's no upside to waiting.

If you just keep up with the daily routines and follow the basic rules of housekeeping, it's really easy to *Clean Like a Man*. Then *keeping* your home clean and tidy becomes a simple matter of ongoing maintenance.

miscellaneous stuff as possible as long as you have the mojo going. While waiting for one thing, do another. Some examples:

* Hungry-Man dinner in the microwave? Use that five minutes to sponge off kitchen counters or sweep the floor.
* Load of laundry going? See if you can get the downstairs rumpus room picked up before the rinse cycle begins.
* TV commercial time? Dust the coffee table, brush the dog fur off the couch cushions, or maybe even brush the dog itself.
* During the evening news, sort the mail, wipe off the kitchen counters, or spot-clean carpet, floor, or appliances.
* While waiting for the coffee to drip, dampen a sponge and wipe out the spatters inside the microwave.

DON'T WASTE A MOVE

This is a first cousin of multitasking. Be a perpetual-motion machine and always be thinking about how to double up on your accomplishments. For example, if your kitchen counters require a light once-over: spray cleaning solution with your left hand, and wipe it up with a rag or a sponge in your right. Or when going upstairs, grab something that belongs there and take it.

Try never to waste a trip, a moment, or a movement. Always think about achieving something "extra" (which is easier when you've set that time limit and you're focused).

Like a shark, keep moving, as if you were a predator of the deep and dirt was chum.

TUNE IN

Use your Walkman—next to the vacuum, it's your most valuable cleaning accessory.

SEND OUT INVITATIONS

That's right, schedule a party at your place. To avoid the shame of having your friends or family enter a messy house, you'll be forced to make sure it's at least moderately clean. Once those invites get jammed in the mail, you've set your own deadline and created the incentive to meet it.

GETTING
GEARED UP
Housecleaning Tools of Thumb

In most manly pursuits, there's nothing better than a good tool well used. This chapter lists the basic housecleaning equipment a guy should have: what you need, where to find it, and how to buy it. Please note that a HAZMAT suit is not on the list.

Vacuum Cleaner

My dog hates and fears the vacuum cleaner. But I consider this machine to be every bit as much "man's best friend" as canines are. Your vacuum represents the most substantial investment you'll make in any housekeeping tool. Not surprisingly, it's also the device that will help you make one of the biggest, fastest dents in your housework . . . which is the bottom line when you want to *Clean Like a Man*. With a vacuum that packs the right features you can clean loose dust and dirt off everything from the ceiling all the way down to carpets and bare floors.

So to help you make a good decision on selecting your vacuum and then use it to maximum advantage, here's a brief primer.

VACUUM CLEANER TYPES

UPRIGHT VACUUMS

These are the stand-up types with a bag and a wraparound storage cord on the handle; a motor and a whirling brush are inside a flat housing that sweeps back and forth across the carpet on wheels. If memory serves, June Cleaver used one. An upright is the best choice if you have lots of carpeting. Its rotating "beater-bar" brush whiplashes dirt out of carpet fibers, then the motor sucks it in. This vacuum cleaner works well, but not great, on bare floors (but its performance is improved when you use extra brush attachments that come with many models).

Be sure to get an upright that has a *built-in hose* (or at least an attachable one) and *attachments* for special cleaning jobs, like tubular extensions for off-the-floor vacuuming, dust brushes for bare floors and counters, upholstery tools, and crevice tools.

Uprights are more compact and easier to store if you live in a tight space. Price range: $100 to $1,000+. You can get all the quality and features you need in an upright vacuum for $150 to $350. Plus there are lots of used models around at thrift stores and shops that specialize in vacuum sales and repair.

CANISTER VACUUMS

These are the beetlelike models on wheels with a protruding hose extension. You pull the body behind you on wheels as you vacuum your way around the room. Canisters with a twirling beater bar brush in their "power nozzle" (the business end of the hose that actually vacuums surfaces) do a very capable job of cleaning carpets. A canister model is a better choice than an upright if you need to clean more wood and tile floors, get underneath low furniture, and vacuum carpeted stairs because the power nozzle with the beater-bar brush is lighter and more maneuverable. Cords retract for storage. Price range: $200 to more than $1,000.

HANDHELD COMPACT VACUUMS

Some have cords, some have batteries, and some recharge when you plug them into wall outlets. They're great for small, on-the-spot cleanups and cheap enough for you to have several. Hand vacs are handy and easy to use, as opposed to the relative ordeal of hauling out and setting up an upright or a canister just to clean a minor mess. On the downside, they don't have the power of their bigger brothers, nor do most of them have the hose and attachments that give uprights and canisters such cleaning versatility. Price range: $25 to $80.

ROBOTIC VACUUMS

Only one has gained any sort of toehold in the marketplace: the Roomba. It has that space-age shape, low-slung enough to get underneath furniture like chairs, beds, coffee tables, and even spaces where canister extensions might not be able to squeeze into. You just punch the on button and the Roomba begins to circle and crisscross the room, vacuuming as it goes. If it hits a wall or a piece of furniture, it spins free and keeps going. Thanks to a padded bumper, Roomba won't cause any damage to woodwork. It even has a side brush that sweeps debris away from edges and into its path. This robotic model is fairly inexpensive (about $200) and sounds like a candidate for the *Clean Like a Man* Hall of Fame, but you have to send it to the manufacturer for servicing. If you must own one, however, Roomba is available at Brookstone, Sharper Image, and Hammacher Schlemmer.

Basic Tips for Purchasing a Vacuum Cleaner

INVEST IN A GOOD ONE

A crappy machine makes cleaning unpleasant. I have a couple of upright models, one a fairly deluxe machine kept on the main floor and, for the smaller upstairs, an old but functional unit I picked up at a thrift store. There's less to clean up there anyway (because, remember: dirt and dust fall).

You can spend as little as $100 for an adequate model or over a grand for one that is way beyond what any guy needs. There's a point of diminishing returns among price, cleaning features, and quality that tops out around $350. In general, the better midpriced upright or canister models will clean up to a man's standards, if not exceed them.

ZERO IN ON THE VACUUM YOU NEED

Consider your cleaning situation. Got lots of carpeting? An upright is probably best, but many canisters with power nozzles perform well. Got lots of above-the-floor stuff like dusty door and window frames, ceiling corners prone to cobwebs, window blinds? Lots of wood or tile floors, or stairs? A canister is your better choice—but again, an upright with a hose attachment would be fine. Confused? Sorry. Both uprights and canisters can do a good job for most situations, as long as they have the essential features.

LOOK FOR THE RIGHT FEATURES

Once you've determined what *kind* of machine you need, get a model with the following features, minimum.

FLEXIBLE "EXTENSION HOSE" ATTACHMENT

This hose is critical, because it lets you clean above the floor, reach into corners, vacuum upholstery surfaces, dust lamp shades, and *much* more with different nozzle attachments. Some newer models have a hose built right into the machine.

MANUAL PILE-HEIGHT ADJUSTMENT

Allows you to match the height of the rotor brush to the carpet's pile (thickness) for more effective cleaning.

ON-BOARD TOOLS

Most of the units with hoses also come with specially designed nozzles that attach to the end of the hose:

* *Small, round utility brush* with long, soft bristles for dusting things like picture frames, windowsills, lamp shades, books, corners, and baseboards in rooms with hard-surface floors
* *Bigger brush* with soft, medium-length bristles for dusting and cleaning big swaths of horizontal space, such as entire wood or tile floors, wooden stairways, walls, ceilings, countertops, pianos, and bookshelves

* *Upholstery attachment* with a stiff, short-bristled brush for getting dust and pet hair off cloth chairs and couches
* *Crevice tool* for getting up close to baseboards in carpeted rooms and reaching into tiny nooks and crannies

EXTRA-CREDIT VACUUM FEATURES

If you want to spend major ching on an upscale vacuum cleaner, you can get features like those below. They're nice, but don't worry: A guy can live without most of them.

DIRT SENSOR

A light signals when the vacuum is no longer picking up dirt (telling you that, theoretically, the carpet is clean).

FULL BAG INDICATOR

A light tells you when the bag is full and ready to change. The bag doesn't have to be completely full, just enough so that efficiency is diminished.

STRATEGIC MANEUVER Easy Vacuum Extras

If you have an upright vac with a hose attachment, buy one or two *extra* lengths of hose and a few additional hard-plastic extension wands (tubes). The extra hose extends the vacuum's cleaning range, so you don't have to take the machine everywhere you go. The tubes let you stand comfortably while vacuuming uncarpeted floors, and make it easier to reach on top of cupboards, ceiling fan blades, the fridge, up into ceiling corners for cobwebs, and more. Both hoses and tubes can often be found at any secondhand store and cost just a buck or two each. Almost all of them fit together and easily clamp onto your vacuum's built-in hose; the hose's ridges usually provide all the "grip" required to hold one piece snugly to another, so you probably won't need to tape them.

ON-OFF BRUSH SWITCH

Lets you turn off the twirling beater brush on uprights or canisters when you're cleaning bare floors, so that only the suction is operating.

SUCTION-CONTROL SWITCH

Decreases suction for fragile or special items like drapes and blinds.

SELF-PROPELLING

Makes each forward/backward sweep easier by providing extra "push." However, machines with this feature are heavier and tougher to haul up and down stairs.

HEPA FILTER

HEPA stands for "high-efficiency particulate air," a filtering feature now available on even many midpriced units. Made of densely packed glass fibers, these filters remove very tiny particulates that might become airborne. The filter is nice, but it's not essential if you have no allergies. And the benefits of a HEPA system are canceled out if a lot of dust and allergens fly back into the air when you empty the vacuum—which can happen with "bagless" models (see below).

QUIETER MOTORS

You'll never find "silent," but try to compare noise when shopping. There are differences that mostly correlate to the quality of the machine. Canisters tend to be quieter than uprights.

LONGER CORD

This will extend your nonstop cleaning range. If the cord is too short—and many are—you'll spend too much time plugging and unplugging the vacuum as you go from room to room. A definite momentum-buster.

BAGLESS

Some vacs now have a drumlike container that collects vacuumed dirt, instead of bags that you have to replace when they fill up. You just remove it occasionally, empty it, and put it back in. While this sounds convenient, the bagless technology is not yet perfected in many models: Removing and emptying the containers can create a dirty mess and produce airborne dust.

WHERE TO BUY YOUR VACUUM

For the best prices, you'll find dozens of brand-name models at stores like Sears, Target, Wal-Mart, Costco, and Sam's Club. There are also many online sources, with some of the best deals at www.brandsmall.com. For consumer reviews and ratings on vacuums (and lots of other merchandise), plus where to find them, click your way to www.epinions.com.

Other Must-Have Cleaning Tools

COTTON CLEANING CLOTHS

There's no substitute for cotton rags when it comes to dusting, washing windows, and cleaning countertops. They're tops where absorbency, streak-free drying, and environmental considerations are concerned. Paper towels are another viable option—very convenient, but not reusable. Synthetic fabrics like polyester don't absorb moisture or pick up dust. Wool or silk, while natural fabrics, are not optimal either, for the same reasons. Cotton is the only kind of cloth to have.

A cotton terry washcloth is the ideal thickness, texture, and size for manly cleaning, but rags that are larger (an old towel) or smaller (an old gym sock) are fine as long as they're cotton. I recommend using white or light-colored cloths so you can tell when they're dirty.

You can purchase packs of cotton cleaning cloths at home, hardware, and discount stores, but you probably have plenty of old cotton sweatshirts, terry bath towels, and socks that you can just cut to size and utilize.

BROOMS

You'll need at least one large stand-up model, usually called a corn broom, and smaller ones will also do the job. One per floor of your house is desirable. You'll also want to have several whisk brooms for mini jobs: stairs, chairs, upholstered furniture. Get a push broom with heavy-duty bristles for the garage and the driveway. And have a dustpan near each broom.

Another manly option is a carpet sweeper, a simple, nonmotorized type of vacuum (or a complicated, mechanized broom, if you want to come at it that way) that's very quick and convenient for small jobs. It's quiet, too. You just push it over the area you want to clean and it whips dirt into the built-in dustpan, which you empty occasionally.

PLASTIC BUCKETS

Have several sizes for different uses: one for carrying cleaning supplies and equipment from one place to another, one in the laundry room, one in the garage for washing the car, and so on. The one you use for housecleaning should ideally be divided into two compartments: one side for cleaning solutions, the other for clean water you can use to rinse sponges and rags, which helps to keep your detergent water cleaner longer. Or you can use one side for clean rags, and the other for dirty ones after they've been used.

SPONGES

Slobs that we are, how can men not love sponges? You can buy a twelve-pack of cheap ones at your local drugstore or supermarket, and these will probably be just fine for the light duty most guys will require. But purchase just a few good sponges, too.

One or two of the bigger cellulose sponges will be ideal for jobs like large floor areas or your car. Then get a half-dozen smaller sponges and stash them in places you'll need them most: bathroom and kitchen. I recommend the ones that have the textured nylon scrubbing surface on one side. Scotch-Brite sponges by 3M are the best; the white nylon backing on these sponges is less abrasive than the green backing, so use the white ones for surfaces that are more prone to scratching. Rinse and wring out sponges after every use, run them through a dishwasher cycle after every few uses, and throw them away when they fray to the point of being ineffective.

HOME **MAN**AGEMENT TIP
Swiffers, ReadyMops, and More

Disposable mops are terrific *Clean Like a Man* tools because you can just reach for one to swipe away dust bunnies, spot-clean a spill, or remove salsa spills from wood or tile floors without goofing around with buckets and dirty water. The basic ones are Procter & Gamble's Swiffer and S.C. Johnson's Pledge Grab-it, both dry mops. The second generation includes the wet mops Swiffer WetJet and Clorox ReadyMop, for more serious cleanups. All have disposable cloth pads that you can change in a jiffy.

All of these mops get the job done, but you should be aware of the differences between them so you can choose the features you prefer. After trying each model, I would go with one of the two wet mops, because they get both dust *and* dirt off floors; dry models remove dust only. The wet mops can also be used dry. You shouldn't use the spray solution on a wooden floor.

Here's a mophead-to-mophead comparison of the wet models:

SWIFFER WETJET
Comes with 34 ounces of cleaning solution, six cleaning pads, and four AA batteries that spray the solution. A year's supply of replacement pads and refill solution will cost about $78 (based on mopping a 15 × 20-foot floor once a week).

CLOROX READYMOP
Comes with 24 ounces of cleaning solution and eight cleaning pads. The solution sprays when you squeeze a trigger on the handle. A year's supply of replacement pads and refill solution will cost about $115 (for the 15 × 20-foot floor, mopped weekly).

PLASTIC SPRAY BOTTLES

Fill your spray bottles with cleaning liquids that you buy in bulk, like glass cleaner, or use them for making solutions of products that can be diluted with water, like ammonia, Lysol, or Pine-Sol. Spray bottles are unbeatable for spritzing solutions onto countertops, appliances, glass, and even floors to dissolve dirt and wipe it up. In fact, spritz-and-wipe is *Clean Like a Man*'s recommended cleaning method whenever possible, because it's so much easier than carrying around a heavy bucket of dirty, sloshing water.

You can purchase spray bottles in a range of sizes from home and hardware stores for $2 or $3 apiece. Cheaper ones won't last. Typically, guys will want to reuse the spray bottles that all your other store-bought cleaning solutions came in. If so, refill each bottle only with the same solution that came in it. Using the container for a different solution is not recommended.

MOPS

Get a good sponge mop with an attached device that squeezes out water so that you can lightly (and quickly!) "damp-mop" a floor. Make sure the sponge head is replaceable (a lot of them aren't). And purchase a couple of replacement sponge heads when you buy the mop itself to avoid having to run out and get one, which will probably break your cleaning momentum.

You probably don't need one of those large string mops for small household tasks. They require a big bucket with a special attachment to wring them out. Too much trouble.

BRUSHES

There are several kinds to have for different uses:

* *Toilet brushes*, one per bathroom, with a discreet holder for each. Use to clean and sanitize the toilet. You may want to keep it under the sink.
* *Tile brushes* with stiff bristles and a handle on top. You can grab the handle and really apply some torque when scrubbing grout (the cementlike filler between tiles) or the water spots and mineral deposits on shower walls and in the tub.

✳ *Old toothbrushes,* which are ideal for small jobs in tight spaces around faucets and stove knobs or along the edge of the sink where it meets the counter, where extra reach is required.

FEATHER DUSTERS

Don't laugh. I'll admit that feather dusters (also called dust wands) seem a little like a prop for the Village People, but these things are great. Most models are made of a cotton candy–like wad of artificial fibrous material attached to the end of a stick, which is perfect for dusting. There are short-handled dusters, but the smart move is to get one with a handle that telescopes out to 4 or 5 feet like a golf-ball retriever, so you can reach up to dust cobwebs from the ceiling, the tops of those overhead room-fan blades, and your mooseheads and mounted fish.

DESIGNER DUST CLOTHS

Prepackaged, disposable dust cloths made of poly fabric that has electrostatic properties are swell for quick cleanups, like grabbing up dust, pet fur, and light amounts of ash, soot, and dirt. The best two on the market are Swiffer and Pledge Grab-it. Both work like cotton cloths spritzed with Pledge or Endust, but you use them dry for light dusting of floors, furniture, computer screens, and the like. When you're finished, just toss them away and buy new ones. They're convenient, but if you're on a budget, you are nickeled-and-dimed to the tune of about $3 for an eight-pack, while cotton cloths are washable, reusable, and more economical.

CARRYALL FOR TOOLS AND SUPPLIES

Also called a Mobile Cleaning Unit (MCU), this device can take many forms: a tool belt, a bucket with double compartments, a cardboard box, a kid's wagon . . . whatever works for you. I prefer a lightweight plastic utility basket with handles, about 12 inches wide by 18 inches long—very similar to shopping baskets—available in most housewares departments. It should be sufficient for all the supplies you'll need for any cleaning expedition, except for your broom, mop, and vacuum cleaner.

MANDATORY ADVICE
Your Basic Cleaning Kit

Here's what to have in your MCU:

* Windex

* A disinfectant cleaner like Lysol

* All-purpose spray-on cleaner like Formula 409 or Orange Clean

* Pledge or Endust

* Soft Scrub or a powder abrasive (Comet for tough jobs, Bar Keepers Friend for light duty)

* Feather duster

* Cotton cloths or rags

* Multipurpose scrubbing brush

* One or two small sponges (with a textured scrubbing surface on one side)

* Whisk broom

* Small dustpan

* Old toothbrush

* Rubber gloves

Have close at hand:

* Long-handled broom, Swiffer, or ReadyMop

* Vacuum cleaner

* Vacuum hose and nozzle attachments

* Walkman with headphones

OTHER MANLY CLEANING TOOLS

SQUEEGEE

To clean both your outdoor windows and your shower walls. When it comes to minimizing moisture (and a mildew-friendly environment) in your shower enclosure, a squeegee is easier to use after every shower than towels. The size most useful for windows is 15 to 18 inches, and a minimum of 12 inches for shower tiles.

RUBBER GLOVES

To protect your hands from harsh chemicals. Buy a size bigger than your hands so they will be easier to take off even if they get wet inside from an accidental slosh.

PLUNGER

To unclog plugged-up drains and toilets.

SMALL FOAM RUBBER MAT

To kneel on when you're doing those near-the-floor chores or any activity that involves kneeling. You'll find them in garden stores.

WALKMAN

To make cleaning as entertaining as possible. CD and MP3 players or a cordless phone with an earplug attachment will also work.

DON'T STAY HOME WITHOUT 'EM
Cleaning Products

*"I love the smell of Windex
Multi-Surface Kitchen & Glass Cleaner
in the morning."*

Most books on housekeeping begin with lengthy recipes for mixing common household products—mainly white vinegar and baking soda—to create all sorts of homemade cleaning solutions. This may save a few pennies, but is it really worth the trouble? You never see janitors fooling around with baking soda or popping bottles of club soda to pull off what Wisk, Clorox, Windex, Orange Clean, and Lime-A-Way already do perfectly well.

There are dozens of cleaning products on the shelves of every hardware store, supermarket, drugstore, and home-improvement outlet in the United States (and most other countries in the world). *Clean Like a Man* highly recommends top-quality, brand-name products for several reasons:

* They're specially formulated for specific cleaning tasks.
* They come in handy containers that make application easy.
* The cheap products are probably cheap for a reason: low quality and poor results.

* The best ones are really not that expensive.
* If the well-known brands weren't good, they wouldn't have been on the market for decades.

What's more, almost all the labels on these products carry a toll-free help-line number you can call to get cleaning advice from a live human being who really knows what she (or he) is talking about. For tips on these help lines, see pages 215–216.

Don't get me wrong—homemade concoctions of baking soda, vinegar, and ammonia can be useful in certain situations. In fact, they're listed below as optional supplies. But the easiest way to go (and therefore the *Clean Like a Man* way) is to invest in premixed, prepackaged, good-to-go products.

MANDATORY ADVICE
Avoid Chemical Reactions

A word to the wise: *Never, ever mix cleaning solutions together!* You can produce chemical reactions that create harmful fumes or skin-burning substances. For example, adding ammonia to chlorine bleach might seem like a great idea, but the combination will produce fumes that can literally burn your sinuses and eyes. Other mixtures may be more benign. But when in doubt (and with housekeeping, men are *always* in doubt), don't take chances.

Whenever you're using chemical cleaners, it's wise to put that macho attitude on the back burner and wear rubber gloves. If you're working with solutions you have to mix in buckets and put your hands into, play it safe. Also, take care not to slosh any in your eyes and keep the room well ventilated (windows or doors open, or an exhaust fan turned on). And again: *Never* mix any two chemicals together.

Essential Cleaning Products

WINDEX

This *Clean Like a Man* essential is *almost* an all-purpose cleaner (now there is Windex Glass & Surface Cleaner, and there are many other versions of the product for different purposes and with various aromas). It does windows, mirrors, picture glass, countertops, stovetops, most appliance exteriors from refrigerator to toaster, aluminum and porcelain sinks, chrome tub and sink fixtures, enamel, ceramic tile, vinyl, and granite.

Windex is proof that you don't need a lot of cleaning supplies, just a few good all-purpose ones. And this is my favorite.

While it doesn't replace disinfectant cleaners for killing bacteria, it's good to use for kitchen counters, nonwood cutting boards, and other food-prep surfaces where microbes aren't welcome.

An ammonia-and-water solution does most of the same things just as well as Windex, but Windex smells much better and you don't have to mix anything.

Don't use Windex on Plexiglas, wood, fabrics, or for the Lexan windows on your private helicopter. Its active ingredient, isopropanol, is great for other cleaning tasks, but it tends to make plastic and Plexiglas surfaces dull, dry, and brittle, and it simply isn't made for cleaning fabrics.

DISINFECTING CLEANER

Have a *disinfecting all-purpose cleaner* such as Lysol, Clorox Clean-Up, Pine-Sol Cleaner & Antibacterial, or Fantastik Antibacterial in your kit. These products not only help you remove grime and dirt, but also kill germs on kitchen counters, bathroom sinks, tubs and showers, cutting boards . . . any surface areas where you want germs dead.

For maximum kill ratio, let your surfectant (the technical name for this stuff) sit for five to ten minutes after spraying it on. It also deodorizes. And while I've never liked the aroma of regular Lysol, I find the lemon-scented version pleasant.

ALL-PURPOSE CLEANER

There are several good products in this category: better than Windex for greasy cleaning jobs but not as good as Windex for glass. They're formulated to tackle grimy jobs like range hoods but are also very effective for sinks, countertops, appliances, toilets, garbage bins, and removing fingerprints from painted walls. All-purpose cleaners handle grease and general cleaning, too; you can dilute them with water or use right out of the bottle. Good all-purpose cleaners include Mr. Clean, Orange Clean, Formula 409, Fantastik, Pine-Sol, and Lysol Pine.

PLEDGE

This aerosol is the real deal for dusting and polishing wood furniture. It removes dust, fingerprints, and smudges, leaving a nice luster. Just spray it on a clean cotton cloth and wipe it across the

HOME **MAN**AGEMENT FACTOID
Coming Clean on Antibacterial Soaps

Most of us take just five seconds or less to wash our hands (it's true: time yourself). But the germ-killing agent in antibacterial soaps requires several minutes of contact on your skin to be effective. So, surprisingly, regular soaps keep germs off you just as effectively as those highly touted antibacterial soaps. In one study, Columbia University's School of Nursing surveyed hundreds of New York City homemakers. Half used ordinary liquid soaps for a year; the other half used antibacterial soaps. At the end of the study, everyone's hands were cultured, and it was a flat-footed tie: Both groups had the same amount of bacteria on their hands, about 300,000 (it's normal to have 1 million or more bacteria on your hands at any given time). Any difference in performance was chalked up to the amount of time people washed their hands.

surface. There's also a Pledge formulation for wood and glass furniture, which makes cleaning items that use both materials (many coffee tables, for instance) a one-step process. Pledge smells great, too. So even if you don't dust, you might want to spray it around just for the effect.

ENDUST

This aerosol polishes wood furniture but is more specifically geared to dusting than Pledge. Spray it on your cotton cloth, then dust. When you spritz some on your broom bristles, dust and dirt sweep up more easily. Plus, Endust slickens up shower tiles to prevent soap buildup and water spots and also makes it easier to clean grease spatters off walls near the stove. Just spray it onto these surfaces every few weeks, then wipe off with a cloth. You'll enjoy faster, easier cleanups in the future.

BATH AND SHOWER CLEANER

These products fight soap scum and mildew in the bathtub, shower curtain, and shower enclosure. Just spray on the tiles, the glass doors, or inside the tub after showering to keep mildew and soap buildup at bay. There's no need to scrub or wipe anything down after you spray, so these cleaners get the *Clean Like a Man* seal of approval. (After showers, wipe water droplets off walls with a towel or squeegee before spraying the product on.)

If some scum or mildew does happen to appear, spray it down with Tilex Mildew Remover, Tilex Soap Scum Remover, Scrubbing Bubbles, Comet Bathroom, or Lysol Daily Shower Cleaner. None require scrubbing. Very cool.

Keep a spray bottle right in the shower or in an adjacent bathroom cabinet. And be sure to turn the bathroom exhaust fan on whenever you use it: Tilex fumes can be pretty strong.

LIME-A-WAY

Lime-A-Way dissolves mineral and calcium residue that is the result of hard water, which you probably have if your soaps and shampoos don't lather well and there's a white, crusty buildup around your faucets. It also helps remove those semipermanent-

MANDATORY ADVICE
Be Careful When Using Chlorine Bleach

While it has stain-removal and sanitizing capabilities, bleach is intended primarily as a laundry additive, not a cleaning agent. It has to be diluted in water, but even then, it can burn ugly white spots into any colored fabric (like your favorite jeans). The only place you should use it outside the laundry room may be to clean mildew off bathroom tile and grout, but only after all other methods (described in Chapter 9) have been attempted.

looking water spots on shower doors, as well as buildup on shower heads and fixtures; to a lesser degree, it gets rid of rust.

SOFT SCRUB LIQUID GEL

This is a mild abrasive gel that's relatively easy on surfaces. It contains bleach, but it won't burn out your sinuses, which is always a plus. Use it to erase stains on surfaces where you'd rather not use a harsh abrasive cleanser that might scratch: tubs and tile, toilets, kitchen and bathroom countertops, sinks, and stovetops. It is strong enough to remove soap scum and semi-tough water spots in the tub and the shower.

SPOT CLEANER

Chili, salsa, and pizza have a way of getting all over the place, so every MCU should carry some type of spot cleaner for carpets, rugs, and upholstery. There are countless varieties for every imaginable spot and stain (pet accidents, grease, food, mud, and so on), but I prefer Resolve or OxiClean. Other brands I can recommend are Capture, Krud Kutter, Formula 409 Carpet Cleaner Spray, and Spot Shot for carpets and rugs, and Carbona for upholstery.

Directions always tell you to first test on an inconspicuous area for colorfastness; then remove any "solid residue" with a spoon or a sponge, spray the soiled area, let stand, and finally blot (don't rub or scrub) from the outside edges of the stain inward to avoid spreading it.

MIRACLE POWDER OR URBAN LEGEND?
Blowing the Lid Off Baking Soda

There are very few housecleaning books that don't hype baking soda as the miraculous do-all powder. And maybe it is. According to the Arm & Hammer Baking Soda website, it's supposed to deodorize things (rugs, cutting boards, refrigerators, garbage cans, dishwashers, drains), whiten your laundry and your teeth, act as a gentle abrasive for scratchable surfaces, remove grease and oil stains from the garage floor, clean hands, clear clogged drains, treat bug bites and poison ivy, polish pots and pans, extinguish grease and electrical fires, and remove stains from coffeepots and cups, just to name a few things on a seemingly endless list.

I've used baking soda, a mild natural alkali, for a few things, and I admit that it does work pretty well. Once, I quickly cleared a very clogged drain by pouring in $1/2$ cup baking soda, then chasing it with $1/2$ cup white vinegar (it fizzed impressively), and, a few minutes later, a kettle of boiling water. Worked like a charm.

The uses of baking soda will be defined at appropriate points throughout this book. There's no harm in using it in cleaning situations where it works, like most of the ones listed above.

Best of all, baking soda is cheaper than dirt. Literally. Ten pounds of baking soda will run you about $4 at a large discount store; ten pounds of potting soil is around $5.

Optional Supplies

ABRASIVE CLEANSER

Comet and Ajax are the best-known brands. Just add a little water to the powder to make a paste for scrubbing tough rust stains, mineral deposits, and the like. I emphasize *tough:* You don't want to use this stuff on any surfaces that may be delicate—porcelain, tiles, stainless-steel sinks, glass, mirrors—because it *will* scratch and take the shine out of surfaces. And you do want to wear rubber gloves.

Bar Keepers Friend is a milder powder alternative that can be safely utilized on fiberglass, glass cooktops, stainless steel, porcelain, tile, even copper and brass.

And the kindest, gentlest, and probably cheapest cleanser of all is baking soda, which is usually effective for polishing or removing stains on countertops, porcelain, cookware, or plastic dishes. Just put $1/4$ cup or so into a small container, keep adding water a little at a time until it mixes up into a smooth paste, apply it to what you're cleaning, let it work for at least a few minutes, then scrub it away with a rag or a Scotch-Brite sponge.

SOAP AND WATER IN A SPRAY BOTTLE

A few drops of plain dishwashing detergent mixed with 16 to 20 ounces of water in a spray bottle makes a great all-purpose cleaner for lightly soiled surfaces like countertops, tile floors, stovetops, and appliances. You can even use it to spot-clean random drops of tomato sauce or Pepsi from the carpet. But don't use too much soap: It might clog the sprayer mechanism.

AMMONIA-WATER SPRITZER

I'm not a huge fan of ammonia, but $1/8$ to $1/4$ cup or so in 1 quart water is an inexpensive alternative to Windex. It does a fine job on windows and other glass surfaces even though its pungent fumes leave a lot to be desired. Stronger ammonia-water solutions can clean grease, stovetops, range hoods, and ovens.

WHITE VINEGAR–WATER SPRITZER

Vinegar is not really a cleaner, but it's a good mildly acidic rinsing agent. Adding 1/2 cup white vinegar to about 1 quart water makes an all-purpose, light-duty cleaning spritzer that's especially practical in the kitchen, where you might not want to use strong chemicals around food-preparation areas. For quick cleanups, just spray onto counters and the stovetop, inside the microwave, and even on tile or vinyl floors.

STRATEGIC **MAN**EUVER
The Pros and Cons of Industrial-Strength Products

Many commercial-grade cleaners are extremely effective, probably even better than the products sold at the supermarket. Professional cleaners use them because they're very strong and sold in bulk. You might want to consider using them if you don't mind:

* Buying in mass quantities and saving some money
* Storing the big jugs and containers, if you have the space
* Mixing the concentrated liquids with water to get a solution of the proper strength for specific jobs
* Seeing through to the bones in your hand if you happen to slosh some onto yourself, or burning your sinus tissue if you accidentally take a whiff

Don't get me wrong, these products are great, especially if you run a large restaurant, clean grade schools for a living, or reside in a warehouse. It's up to you. If you go this route, you can find commercial cleaning products at janitorial-supply stores, or even price clubs like Costco or Sam's Club. But they're probably overkill for *Clean Like a Man* purposes. The mixing aspect alone requires rubber gloves and either spray bottles, which are fine, or buckets, which we're trying to avoid as much as possible.

4

GETTING DOWN AND DIRTY
How-to Techniques

This chapter covers the Big Three cleaning tasks: vacuuming, dusting, and cleaning windows and glass, which represent most of the housecleaning chores you'll have to tackle. In Part II, *Clean Like a Man* will get into room-by-room specifics, mostly variations on the themes you'll learn here. If you master these skills and keep the Men Commandments from Chapter 1 in mind, you'll always be good to go: to catch a ball game, to play a round of golf, or to enjoy an afternoon Couchmaster workout.

Vacuuming

Vacuum cleaners help a guy *clean a lot and clean it fast*, which is the entire essence of *Clean Like a Man*. They've evolved into true twenty-first-century machines, sporting that sleek, Formula One look and featuring technological advances that can save you many hours of housecleaning time. Once you know how to use this tool, you're ready to *GO, GO, GO!*

ONBOARD TOOLS

Most of the latest vacuum cleaners feature "onboard tools" integrated right into the machine. These include all the specialized cleaning accessories you need, primarily extension tubes and nozzles that can be attached to the flexible hose that comes on all canister models and almost all uprights.

The tubes—rigid pieces about 18 inches long—extend your reach. This is a real boon to MANkind because it lets you clean from the ceiling on down into every nook and cranny of a room. All the proper attachments are at your fingertips, too: the nozzle heads designed for specific jobs, which fit onto the vacuum hose or tubes. They're covered in Chapter 2; here's a quick refresher course, in order of importance:

✳ *Small, round utility brush* for dusting picture frames, doorsills and windowsills, lamp shades, books, and other small items and areas.

✳ *Bigger brush* for dusting and cleaning larger surfaces like wood or tile floors, wooden stairways, tabletops, and pianos.

✳ *Upholstery attachment* with a stiff brush lip for getting dust and pet hair off upholstery.

✳ *Crevice tool* for getting into smaller spaces.

Here's the best way to finesse housecleaning with the vacuum:

1. Attach one or two extension tubes to the hose, and the small utility brush to the end of the tube. Vacuum cobwebs from ceiling corners and dust the tops of door frames, windowsills, appliances, and anything else above eye level.

2. Move to eye level with the same attachments and vacuum dust off lamp shades, books and shelves, tabletops, and other items.

3. Go lower, using the same attachments for noncarpeted stairs, low tables, hard floors underneath furniture, and baseboards.

4. For bare floors, slide the bigger dust brush (it's 9 to 12 inches long and 2 to 3 inches wide) onto the end of the hose or the extension tube. Then draw it back and forth over the floor to loosen and suck up dust and dirt. You can also take a broom and sweep debris to one spot, usually a corner, then vacuum it up.

5. For carpets, remove the nozzle and put the hose back in its regu-

lar position. Then set your pile-height adjustment according to the carpet's pile (fiber length), usually "1" for the shortest carpets and higher numbers for the more plush ones. *Vacuum slowly,* back and forth, going over high-traffic areas more thoroughly because soil works its way deeper into the carpet there.

Theoretically, the only time you have to stop vacuuming is to change the bag in the machine. Some models don't even have bags anymore, just containers you pull out, empty, and put back in. Here are more tips and techniques to help you do the best job in the time you have:

* *Get a model with a longer cord,* or attach an extension cord. Some cords are ridiculously short, so you're continually plugging and unplugging as you move from room to room.
* *Use small, portable handheld vacuums* for quick cleanups. The Dustbuster and the Dirt Devil brands come to mind. Many models are available with your choice of features: cords, batteries, or plug-in recharging.
* *Change bags fairly often.* A machine's cleaning power starts suffering when the bag becomes about half full, so replace it after that.
* *Avoid "bagless" models.* Emptying their dirt containers can often be messy.
* *Take your time when vacuuming.* The guy at my local vacuum store advised "going slow" to do the most effective job. He also said you should make seven passes over each area for the best results, but this violates the "too Felix" rule.
* *Store several compact vacs* in strategic places: in the bedroom closet, under the bathroom sink, under the kitchen sink.
* *Stay dry.* Don't try to vacuum up wet stuff with a regular vacuum.
* *Vacuum weekly* if you can fit it into your tight schedule. Try to vacuum high-traffic areas like entrances at least once a week. Dirt particles actually work their way down into the carpet, cutting its fibers and shortening its life.
* *Save your instruction manual.* File it so you can always find out what to do if your vacuum belt breaks, or if another troubleshooting scenario comes up.
* *Put mats at all entrances.* They'll keep a lot of shoe-borne dirt from getting into your house.

Dusting

Dust is everywhere, and it is totally relentless—after you clean, it always comes back. So the best you can hope for is to deal with dust as efficiently as possible for the moment, resigned to the fact that it shall return.

WHY DUST?

The obvious reason is plain to see: visual blight. A layer of dust is very unaesthetic, especially when it's so thick you could diagram football plays in it.

Dust is also unhealthy. It will aggravate allergies. It's a pollutant, and if it's floating around the room and through air ducts—which it does constantly—you'll breathe it into your lungs.

Dust is also destructive and expensive. Look at your furnace filter the next time you change it. More than a few months' buildup of dust and airborne particles in effect "smothers" your furnace, cutting down heating/cooling efficiency and possibly damaging your unit. And thick dust on your refrigerator's cooling coils reduces its efficiency and could wreck that machine, too.

DUSTING RULES

1. Dust before you vacuum the floor, not after.
2. Start high, often as high as the ceiling, using your vacuum or extendable dust wand (feather duster) and work your way down to the floor.
3. When dusting by hand, use only cotton cloths. Synthetic fabrics have very little pick-up power or absorbency.
4. Dampen your dust cloth with either a light spritz of water or a dusting and furniture polish product like Pledge or Endust. This way, dust adheres to the cloth and you're not just pushing it from one place to another.

HOW TO USE DUSTING TOOLS

VACUUM CLEANER

Invaluable for dusting. But whether you use an upright or a canister model, it won't be effective for dusting without a flexible, extendable hose, a couple of rigid tubes, and some brush attachments—all discussed earlier. With this setup, you can do a mind-blowing job of dusting every corner and surface in a room plus items like blinds, lamp shades, floors, and more, just by changing your attachments. To use for dusting, take your machine's flexible hose and add one or two rigid extension tubes to give yourself some reach. Place the appropriate attachments onto the end of the extensions for various jobs:

SMALL ROUND UTILITY BRUSH. Use for ceiling and wall corners, smaller counters and tabletops, lamp shades, window blinds, and collectibles; the top edges of picture frames, doorways, and window frames; baseboards and heat duct grilles.

BIGGER BRUSH. Use for larger counters and tabletops, wood and tile floors, and the tops of refrigerator and cupboards.

CREVICE TOOL. Use to get into tight spaces between kitchen appliances and cabinets, along baseboards where they meet carpeting, and so on.

COTTON CLEANING CLOTHS

These are the best of all possible options in the world of wipe-ups, leaving most other rag stock, well . . . in the dust. You can purchase inexpensive white cotton terry hand towels or washcloths in whatever size suits you. They're ultra-absorbent—they don't just push dust around, they grab it up—plus they don't scratch. Their nubby facing is a terrific cleaning texture and they softly envelope uneven surfaces, or fold into a compact pad to sponge off flat areas. They're washable and reusable, which is both economically and environmentally sound. Get lots of white ones so you can tell when they're soiled. Old cloth diapers are a close second, and paper towels are okay, too. Most other fabrics, especially synthetic ones, suck.

To use:

1. Use your cloth open or fold it into a spongelike shape.
2. Spray Pledge or Endust onto it, then wipe over dusty areas. This both grabs dust and polishes furniture surfaces.

3. Launder your cotton cloths with detergent and a little bleach to keep them fresh and sanitized.

DESIGNER DUST CLOTHS

As described in Chapter 2, these prepackaged, disposable cloths have electrostatic properties that attract dust, pet fur, and light soil. The best two, Swiffer and Pledge Grab-it, both work like cotton cloths spritzed with Endust, but you use them dry for quick, light dusting jobs. For floors, they attach securely to mops of the same names. They're convenient but pricey: about $3 for an eight-pack.

DUST WANDS

Made of a wad of fibrous, cotton candy–like material attached to the end of a handle, they pick dust up from surfaces or stir it up so that it falls to the floor, where you can then vacuum it up. Use your dust wand to quickly clean lamp shades, crevices, slats, and intricate carving on furniture. Buy a wand with an extendable, telescoping handle to reach up into places like ceiling corners and the tops of ceiling fan blades.

BROOMS

One long-handled broom per floor, with dustpans or hand vacuums nearby to collect the swept-up debris. A few whisk brooms for stairs, corners, and small counters. Optional: a manual carpet sweeper (described in Chapter 2) that handles small on-the-floor jobs quickly and easily.

DUST MOPS

The traditional kind of this alternative to the vacuum consists of cotton strands on a handle (space-age newcomers include the Swiffer WetJet and Clorox ReadyMop—see page 35 in Chapter 2). They are used mainly to dust big swaths of wood or tile floors but are effective on ceilings and walls as well. Slightly dampen the cloth strands of a traditional dust mop or spray with Pledge or Endust for maximum dusting effect. When you're done, go outside and shake out the dust.

HAIR DRYERS

They are very good for blowing dust off lamp shades and artificial flowers, but to remove dust rather than simply scatter it, use a vacuum with a brush attachment.

PLEDGE AND ENDUST

These products not only enhance the effectiveness of dust cloths and dust mops but also polish wood furniture and make rooms smell great. Just spray some on the surface or on your dust cloth or dust mop, and go to it. In a pinch, use a little water to dampen the cloth or the mop to enhance its dust-attracting power.

SPECIAL DUSTING TASKS

REFRIGERATOR COILS

These coils do all the refrigerator's cooling. They're located at the bottom of most newer models, behind the plastic kick plate that snaps on and off. If the coils are on the back of the fridge, roll it

HOME **MAN**AGEMENT
Where Does Dust Come From?

I've always had an image of tiny, harmless fibers floating into the house on zephyrlike breaths of air. Wherever it originated, dust has always been the ultimate renewable resource, that's for sure.

The dust in your home is indeed partly made up of minuscule fabric fibers, but there's more. It's also composed of the microscopic skin particles and dander shed by most living things, plus bits of ash, pollen from plants and flowers, airborne dirt that's picked up off the ground by wind, construction activity, and traffic, mold and mildew spores, and dust mites. The dust mites are alive, and they're constantly eating all the other stuff.

That said, wouldn't you rather clean dust than breathe it in?

away from the wall to expose them. The coils must be kept relatively dust-free or the fridge will cool less efficiently or break down altogether. Be gentle; the coils are fragile. Reach into the tight space underneath the fridge and wipe dust off with a thin, long-handled bottle brush or a yardstick with a sock attached with a rubber band around one end, or even your car's snowbrush.

BLINDS AND LOUVERED DOORS

To dust the slats, attach your vacuum's small round utility brush, or use a dust wand or a cotton cloth that can be either sprayed with Pledge or Endust, or dampened with water.

DRAWERS

If you have one or more drawers filled with small items, you can either empty the drawer and vacuum it out with your small brush attachment, or leave the items inside and attach a nylon stocking to the vacuum hose nozzle with a rubber band—dirt and small debris will be sucked onto the nylon's surface, and you can then brush it off over a wastebasket. Just make sure the nylon isn't in active rotation in your wife's or girlfriend's wardrobe.

CREVICES AND OTHER TIGHT SPOTS

The crevice tool on your vacuum gets a few inches deep into cracks. You can also use a small, soft paintbrush to whisk dust out into the open. If you have to reach way back into a small opening, attach a sock to a yardstick, a hanger, or a dowel with a rubber band, spray it with Pledge or Endust, and "go deep."

PLANTS

Use a hair dryer set on cool, or just put the plants in the shower and run water over them.

Cleaning Windows and Other Glass

I like cleaning windows, mirrors, glass-topped coffee tables, and the like because the end result is such a pleasure to behold. And it's easy to turn filmy, smudged-up windows and glass into sparkling clean, streak-free, crystal-clear surfaces.

INSIDE WINDOWS, MIRRORS, AND GLASS TABLES

HOW-TO

* Spray on Windex (or an ammonia-and-water solution from a spray bottle).
* Wipe off with cotton cloths or paper towels.
* Repeat if any dust, smudges, or film remains.

TIPS

* For a finishing touch, spray on one more *light* spritz of your solution and wipe with your driest, cleanest cotton cloth.
* Clean windows from the top down.
* Clean large windows in quadrants, one area at a time, instead of the entire window. You'll do a more thorough, streak-free job.
* Don't use newsprint: It leaves a filmy residue on windows, and the ink blackens your hands.

OUTSIDE WINDOWS

EQUIPMENT

* Bucket
* 15- to 18-inch-wide squeegee, ideally with a nylon mesh-covered sponge attached, like the ones you use to clean your windshield at the gas station
* Long or extendable handle for the squeegee; or use a ladder
* Clean, dry cotton terry cloths or rags, or paper towels
* Sponge attachment for the squeegee handle
* Ammonia, dishwashing detergent

HOW-TO

* Put about 1 gallon warm water into a bucket and add 1/2 cup ammonia plus a few drops of dishwashing detergent. Stir to mix.
* Apply the solution to the window with the sponge on your squeegee.
* Squeegee it off from the top down, using vertical strokes that start at the top edge of the window and overlap each other. Wipe the squeegee edge with a piece of terry cloth after each pass.
* Wipe any wet streaks off the windows as you go with a terry cloth or paper towel.

STRATEGIC **MAN**EUVER
Washing Second-Story Windows

Don't have a ladder for your home's upper windows? Try Windex Outdoor Concentrated Cleaner as an easy alternative. It cleans dirt off the windows and leaves surprisingly few streaks. Just attach the container to your garden hose, spray the solution onto your high windows, wait fifteen to thirty seconds, replace the Windex container with your regular hose nozzle, then spray clear water up onto the windows to rinse them. According to the label, it's safe for siding, paint, and shrubs—and it's definitely safer than risking your neck on a tall ladder.

✳ If you don't have a squeegee, apply the solution with a sponge to get the thickest dirt, then dry with a terry cloth. With this method you might want to follow up with a light spritzing of Windex, dried with your terry cloth, to make sure the surface is streak-free.

TIPS

✳ Don't wash windows in the heat of direct sunlight; the solution will dry too quickly and it will streak.
✳ If windows have multiple panes, do the upper ones first and work your way down.
✳ Don't use too much diswashing soap; it will leave a film that you'll have to remove from the window with Windex. Just two or three drops per gallon of water are plenty.

OTHER GLASS

The main active ingredient in Windex and other dedicated glass cleaners (and rubbing alcohol, too) is the solvent isopropanol. It's good for a lot of cleaning chores, but it's hell for some. Windex and similar glass cleaners (especially solutions containing ammonia or alcohol) can damage the following surfaces. Here's how you *should* clean them:

COMPUTER AND TV SCREENS

Use a fabric softener sheet, a cotton cloth, a Pledge Grab-it cloth, or even a coffee filter with cleaning solution made specifically for computer and TV screens sprayed onto the cleaning cloth—*not* directly onto the screen. Don't use Windex or alcohol- or ammonia-based cleaners; they can damage the screen.

PLEXIGLAS

Use only mild soap and water applied with a soft cotton cloth, then dry with a cotton cloth. Do not use alcohol-based solutions like Windex, which will tend to make the surface dry, brittle, and dull.

EYEGLASSES

Apply mild soap and water or a dedicated lens cleaner like Kleen spray solution, then dry lightly with a soft cotton cloth and polish with a silk cloth. Hairspray spots on your glasses don't wipe off easily and can damage the surface. To remove these spots, wash eyeglasses with a mild dishwashing detergent and water, then rinse; the glasses will be sparkling clean.

TELESCOPES AND BINOCULARS

Use a soft cotton cloth, a microfiber cloth, or a coffee filter to clean off smudges and fingerprints. For a more thorough cleaning, apply photographic lens–cleaning fluid to the cloth and clean carefully.

HARD CONTACT LENSES

If conventional means fail, try a little toothpaste (no kidding, it works). But rinse off the toothpaste completely before you put the contacts into your eyes again.

THE ORGANIZATION MAN
A Place (and a Time) for Everything

Because organizing and uncluttering your space are the true cornerstones of good housekeeping, a multitude of very good books has been written on these topics. Unfortunately, most men haven't read any of them. But the "pro" arguments for being organized are undeniable:

* One of the highest-priority cleaning rules is to pick up the place before you begin, so you can see what has to be cleaned.
* Organizing, uncluttering, and downsizing constitute addition by subtraction: With fewer things to maintain, you save time and money—plus there's less to pick up before you clean.
* Uncluttering removes visual pollution and enhances the beauty and serenity of your space. This promotes tranquillity and clarity of mind—like a Japanese Zen garden, except without the rocks and sand.
* Neat and orderly surroundings make it much easier to live a neat, orderly, low-hassle life. You never have to waste time looking for keys, glasses, wallets, receipts, or anything else you need because *you know exactly where things are.* You are always calm

and collected. You are punctual and dependable. You are admired by everyone.

* Devising a simple list or two can do wonders for streamlining your days and making you more efficient. Lists allow you to prioritize chores, consolidate errands, and remember a multitude of easily forgettable (but still important) things.

* A filing system—even a rudimentary one—can help you conquer all the paper that's scattered around.

* Finally, running your life using a basic scheduling system—preferably written on a calendar—means that you'll miss very few appointments, anniversaries, birthdays, baptisms, bar mitzvahs, or dinner dates.

The benefits of being organized go way beyond not having crap strewn everywhere you look. It helps a man save loads of time, space, stress, and money. Believe it: The smart organizing moves you're about to discover can go way beyond simplifying your cleaning efforts—they can help you streamline your entire life.

Master Your Domain (and Your Stuff)

DOWNSIZE AND UNCLUTTER

Getting rid of everything you don't need is smart, but it's tougher than it sounds. Where you draw the line between keeping something and donating or trashing it is ultimately up to you. But here's what happens when you do purge:

* You won't need to clean those extra possessions anymore, saving you oodles of dusting, vacuuming, and maintenance time.

* You have more space to store what you do keep.

* When you're in one of your rare housekeeping moods, it's easier to sustain momentum when you don't have to stop and pick up things.

* You can find things faster: sunglasses, receipts, checkbook, bearer bonds, and so on. No more ten-minute delays to search for your billfold or car keys when you're taking off.

* Your contribution to a local thrift store lets others obtain the items they need for a good price and gives you a charitable tax deduction. (Consult your tax adviser for details.)

HOW ORGANIZED (OR NOT) ARE YOU?

Agree or disagree with the following:

You don't remember the last time you changed the furnace filter.

Agree____   Disagree____

Misplacing your car keys, wallet, glasses, or some other essential happens at least once a week.

Agree____   Disagree____

Sometimes you don't pay a bill on time.

Agree____   Disagree____

Your weekly planner seldom comes out of your briefcase.

Agree____   Disagree____

If someone opened your refrigerator, they'd think that decomposing condiments made up much of the food pyramid.

Agree____   Disagree____

You frequently return from errands and realize you've forgotten something.

Agree____   Disagree____

There doesn't seem to be enough time in a day to do everything you need to do.

Agree____   Disagree____

How many times did you agree with these statements?

0   Congratulations, Felix.

1–2   Not bad but not perfect.

3–4   You have lots of room for improvement.

5 or more   You're very disorganized.

Sometimes, you just have to let go. Still, it's often difficult to part with items that you think have value, whether sentimental, monetary, or utilitarian. Will you ever use it again? Have you enjoyed it lately? Would you grab it if the house were on fire? Here are a few rules of thumb to help you decide what you really need and what's just wasting space and gathering dust.

1. Haven't worn it in a year? *Hasta la vista,* baby. Those ties aren't coming back into style. You'll probably never again fit into that sport coat. You didn't like that sweater in the first place. The general guideline is: If you haven't worn a garment in the past twelve months, it shouldn't be taking up space in your closet.

2. Duplicates? How many do you really need? Having multiples of certain items is common, especially in the kitchen (silverware, plates, mugs, and glassware don't count—it's MANdatory to have more than one of each). But if you own several can openers, toasters, rice makers, cap snafflers, and other gadgets, ditch all but your favorite of each. The second most duplicate-prone area is usually your workshop: You probably have several hammers, sets of drill bits, pliers, and who knows how many screwdrivers you don't need.

3. Sentimental value? Have you used or enjoyed it recently? Is it valuable? Will you need it in the future? What has it done for you lately? If the answer is nothing, it goes. You have to draw the line somewhere. Remember, whoever buys it at the thrift store will treasure it. (Maybe.)

4. Don't know why you still have it? Use or lose these things . . . right now: unused keys; expired coupons; outdated phone books; old restaurant guides; unfinished projects; pots, pans, and utensils you haven't used in a year or two; textbooks you'll never open again; old magazine "collections"; old cleaning supplies and cans of paint (both can be considered pollutants, so call your community authorities regarding regulations for their disposal).

5. On the fence? If you come across an item you're not sure about keeping or discarding, I say toss it. But many other books give you some wiggle room. They suggest that if you're uncertain about whether you should keep something, you should toss it into a big cardboard box with everything else that's under review

Clutter Is Costly

The major cause of owning more than one of the same item (can openers, screwdrivers, etc.) is that your place is so disorganized that you can't find what you need, so you go out and buy another one. This waste of time and money highlights a primary benefit of uncluttering and organizing: If you have a place for everything, you'll always be able to find what you need—and you won't have to buy another one.

and date it for six months from today. As you need something from the box, take it out, use it, and put it away elsewhere. But when the six months are up, seal up the box and call Goodwill— it contains things you haven't used and don't need.

BOXING MATCH

Here's a way for you to drive your uncluttering plan forward by deciding what you need and what you don't. Get at least three large boxes and mark them as indicated below. Then take them into a room and throw the appropriate things into them.

1. *Throw away.* This needs very little explanation. In your heart, you know what's just junk and should be trashed.
2. *Give away.* Be honest with yourself: Will the item ever again be useful to you? Does it have such sentimental value that the thought of never seeing it again is unbearable? Or is it a case of "one man's junk is another man's treasure"? Another option here is a garage sale.
3. *Put away.* This is the stuff you decide to keep but not to throw it around the room again. You're going to either stash it in long-term storage or put it "in its place" where it's convenient when you need it but out of sight when you don't.

MANDATORY ADVICE
Store Like Items Together

Use your common sense to decide what items to put into the same container, drawer, or cupboard. Things that have similar purposes should be stored together: tapes, glues, Velcro straps, and other adhesives; paper clips, staplers, pens and pencils, envelopes, stamps, address stickers, and other office supplies; resealable bags, aluminum foil, wax paper, and twist ties. This way, when you say "I need a screwdriver" you'll go to your workshop storage drawer where all your tools, screws, nuts and bolts, sandpaper, etc., should be. Likewise for cleaning supplies—stash all tools, solutions, rags, vacuums, and so on, in one closet.

ORGANIZE IN INSTALLMENTS

Often, because you're looking at mountains of stuff and there isn't enough time to pick it all up and put it away, you don't deal with any of it. Even if you *do* have the time for a massive organizing effort, the prospect of burning up an entire Saturday is depressing. The solutions:

* Don't start an uncluttering project you know you can't finish.
* Take it one step at a time. Set smaller, achievable goals so you'll be able to see your progress and feel good about it.
* Allocate a reasonable amount of time to achieving one goal— spend fifteen minutes today uncluttering or organizing a certain room. You can certainly spare that much time, and you can get a lot done if you have a focused goal.

STRETCH STORAGE SPACE

Here are several easy, inexpensive ways to quickly clean up and organize storage space—and maybe find more of it. (And there are even more smart tips on using closet space in Chapter 10, which covers the bedroom.)

KITCHEN

* Every kitchen has a junk drawer. Empty yours, then insert a plastic divider/organizer from a hardware or discount store. Put all the items you decide to keep into the compartments in a semblance of organization. Toss the real junk away.
* Keep appliances you don't use every day (blender, toaster oven, food processor, etc.) out of sight in cabinets or cupboards. Try to maintain clean, uncluttered kitchen counters; only a coffeemaker, a set of knives, a small TV or radio, and maybe some books on cooking and entertaining should be out.
* Create extra storage behind pantry doors by hanging a see-through shoe holder. Available in the housewares section, it's a great place to keep your cleaning products and tools—you can see everything from Windex to whisk broom at a glance—for at-your-fingertips convenience.
* To utilize a space that's otherwise wasted, install narrow, lipped shelves (available at home and hardware stores) on the inside of cupboard doors to store and display spices and other small items.
* Store your most-used pots, pans, and cooking tools at the front of drawers and cupboards for easy access.
* Go vertical: Insert modular, stackable wire storage drawer units into cupboards to create more vertical storage space for napkins, tablecloths, larger utensils, and more.
* Put mail in a basket or holder on a kitchen counter. It'll be just visible enough to remind you to take care of it, which you should do right away.

BATHROOMS

* Try to avoid lots of knickknacks (or any, for that matter) and bathroom-humor reading material. Make things you *do* need to leave out in the open look organized: a box of tissues on the toilet tank, or a nice box for watches and any other accessories.
* Most grooming items should be stashed under the sink or in the medicine cabinet or in drawers.

HOME **MAN**AGEMENT TIP
Two Good Habits That Go a Long Way

Make the Bed Every Morning
First thing, without fail. While you're at it, maybe straighten up the bedside tables and the counters in the bathroom, each of which only takes a few seconds. It always gets the day off to a good start with the visual impression that everything is in order. After all, "perception = reality" is one of *Clean Like a Man*'s central tenets.

Jam All Dishes and Silverware into the Dishwasher After Eating
With absolutely no visual clutter in or near your kitchen sink, you'll be inspired to keep the counters cleaned and clear. Again, it only takes a few minutes but has a big impact.

* If space is an issue, hang a shoe holder that can store often-used items like a hair dryer, brushes, shaving stuff, and some toiletries on the door.
* If you need even more storage space, the wall behind the toilet is a good place for narrow shelves or an extra cabinet.

CLOSETS

* Explore the farthest reaches of your closets. They may be gold mines that yield both new storage space and an impressive number of giveaway items.
* Transparent plastic storage bins (they come in all sizes) provide see-through storage for out-of-season clothing, extra blankets, sweaters, and more.
* Place old bookcases into closets for instant shelving.
* To keep closet floors clear, hang a shoe rack with pockets on a door, or purchase a shoe-rack kit at your local home or hardware store.

* Make folded sweaters, jeans, and other similar items easier to see by stacking them instead of stuffing them in drawers: Install shelving above the hanger rod. Space the shelves fairly close together (about 12 inches vertically), because piling folded garments too high makes it tough to remove one of the lower items without messing up the entire stack.

GARAGE

* If you have vertical 2 × 4 studs facing inward, cut other 2 × 4s to make shelves in the recesses between them. These easy-to-see rows provide almost limitless storage space where you can keep smaller items neatly organized and out of the way.
* Peg-Board is a superb solution for garage storage. Just nail big sections onto the studs, then add as many hooks, pegs, and hanging containers as you want. There are dozens of different kinds of Peg-Board hardware, and you can easily move them around to hang whatever tools you own.

TURN YOUR SHELVES INTO DRAWERS

Shelves where lots of small items collect are chronic storage problem areas, especially for guys who look right past them: the spices in your kitchen cupboard; all the tools lying around your workshop and scattered on top of your work table; the prescription and vitamin bottles, shaving supplies, cotton balls, Q-tips, colognes, combs, brushes, scissors, nail kit, toothpaste, and other lotions and potions cluttering up your bathroom. The solution is easy and cheap:

* Get rough measurements of all shelves that are so cluttered with small items that you can't see labels to identify them and you always have to paw through everything to locate what you want. Go to your discount, hardware, or home store and purchase containers to hold all that stuff. Create topless "drawers" that sit on the shelves and easily slide in and out, allowing you to see what's inside.
* A plastic dishpan or two is the perfect solution for under the kitchen sink: Its low profile and slideability make it the ideal hopper for dishwashing detergent, spray bottles, and cleansers.

Under the bathroom sink it's just the thing for holding hair dryers, medicine kits, bowl cleaner, shower spray, or extra rolls of toilet paper.

* Stash smaller items in more compact plastic containers like those ice-cube storage bins with the open front, or in see-through plastic shoe boxes, which even have covers. They're great for storing brushes, sponges, and rubber gloves under the kitchen sink.

* A shallow plastic cake pan is perfect for consolidating all those spices in your kitchen cupboard and medicines or toiletries in the bathroom.

* Many different sizes and shapes of small, modular containers are available to slip into drawers as partitions or mini storage bins; slide them into cupboards and shelves as pull-out or stack-up storage. Some are even made to nest together, like the trays in your fishing tackle box.

ONE MORE OPTION: HIRE A PRO

No, not a psychiatrist. (At least not yet.) There are organizing specialists who will actually come into your home and help with everything from uncluttering closets to filing to balancing your checkbook. An expert can look around at what you have, listen to what you want, and make good things happen—long-term solutions to your storage problems, not just stopgap measures. You can find them in the Yellow Pages or newspaper want ads under "Organizing Products & Services." It's a good investment if you really feel overwhelmed.

Streamline Your Life

A guy's life can be complicated. We overload ourselves with appointments to keep, deadlines to meet, flights to catch, games to watch, dates to impress, places to be, and things to do. Here are some ideas to help you squeeze the most out of every minute.

A PLACE FOR EVERYTHING

One rule can simplify a man's life more than any other, and it's older than dirt: "Have a place for everything and everything in its place." It's not just about stuff; it encompasses both space and time.

For items you're likely to need as you go out the door every day, an entryway table or shelf can work wonders:

* Keys: Place on entryway table, or hang them on a small hook or a set of hooks near the door.
* Mail: It can get scattered all over the house unless you corral it (see "Dealing with Mail," below).
* Wallet: It has all your IDs, credit cards, and cash in it. You're not going anywhere without it, so you should never have to search for it.

Form is secondary to function: a decorative table near the front door, a utilitarian ledge near the garage entrance, and a windowsill in the mud room all work well. Train yourself with one or two items at a time. For example, make it a point to put your keys, wallet, or glasses in the same place every day, every time you come in the door. Place your shoes on the rack in your bedroom closet each time you take them off. Hang up your clothes when you get home or get ready for bed. Sort your laundry, fold it, and store it right away.

Just keep putting your most important things in their places; it will become a habit that spills over into the rest of your life, too.

DEALING WITH MAIL

Do you remember that it's time to pay bills only when the stack of envelopes falls over? If you need to stay a little more up to date on your mail, try the OHIO rule: "Only Handle It Once." The theory is that if you keep up with bills, bank statements, and letters on a daily basis, they won't pile up. Try to sort through the mail every day: throw away the junk mail; pay the bills or put them in a dated "tickler" file in your office or appointment book; read your personal letters and answer them if possible; put magazines on the coffee table or bedside table, wherever you read them.

It helps to have a favorite place and time to go through your mail—sitting at your desk, leaning on a kitchen counter, or flopping in your La-Z-Boy when you get home from work. It's also a good idea to put correspondence like letters you intend to answer in a container like a basket placed in a convenient spot. After you've handled all the items in the day's mailbag, throw them away or file them.

OHIO is a great concept on the drawing board, though it's not always possible to practice it in real life. Nevertheless, it's worth a shot: You'll never stop getting mail.

FILE, DON'T PILE

Develop a simple filing system. *Any* method of keeping track of your paperwork is more effective and efficient than none at all. Your system can be as simple as having one folder or envelope marked "Important Docs" with the current year noted, where you tuck all documents related to taxes, insurance, finance, medical, licenses, restraining orders, etc. With it, you'll know where everything is when, for example, the tax man beckons.

Then, at a minimum, add a second folder or envelope for "Receipts" and a third for "Bank." Your biggest folder or envelope will be the one holding receipts. You might want to divide this file into "Regular" and "Tax Deductions." You can split the items above into separate folders (as many as you want): Car, Insurance—

STRATEGIC **MAN**EUVER
How to Get Less Junk Mail

To have your name removed from many direct mailers' lists, write (or just send a postcard) to the Direct Marketing Association, ATTN: Mail Preference Service, Dept. 11630050, P.O. Box 282, Carmel, NY 10512. Include your mailing address and tell them to remove your name and address from circulation.

Don't fill out those "surveys" that come with the mail-in warranty registration cards of items you buy: If you do, the manufacturer will sell your name and purchasing profile to other firms that want to send you junk mail.

STRATEGIC **MAN**EUVER
Cro-Magnon Filing

A friend of mine uses a filing system that's about as rudimentary as it gets, but it has a frightening beauty all its own. He just tosses every receipt, bank statement, and paid bill into one big box marked with the current year. Every January 1 he switches to a new box. "It's not that detailed," he says, "but if I ever need a document from that year, I know exactly where it is: in that box."

Home, Insurance—Auto, Insurance—Medical, 401K, Mortgage (or Rent), and so on. Then get a few "banker's boxes," the sturdy cardboard ones with holes for handles on each side. At the end of each year, put your files in one of them and stash them in the basement or in a remote closet, just so you have your records somewhere. If you keep filling boxes with new files year after year, you'll be covered for tax audits, insurance claims, and any other events that require paperwork.

Leveraging Lists

Most organized, effective people utilize lists. Whether you're swinging through the supermarket, going to the hardware store, or embarking on a busy day at the office, having a list is a survival tool for many guys.

Men are busy people, as you know. Lists help us remember all those small-but-significant things: what items to purchase for meals and projects so we can get everything we need in just one trip; whose birthday it is; when the dry cleaning is supposed to be ready; which tasks are real priorities for the workday ahead; when and where our meetings are scheduled; what time to pick up the dog from his violin lesson and the kids from obedience school. Plus:

* A list helps you *prioritize* deadlines, errands, and appointments. Write down everything you have to do that day, then number everything so you can separate the "gotta-dos" from the "would be nice to dos."

* A list helps you *consolidate* errands: driving downtown or to the mall just once, doing all the shopping you have to do in a single trip instead of in multiple trips over the span of several days.

* A list, even one randomly jotted, helps you *remember* the billions of tiny details that pop into your head and pop out again just as quickly, like that you need toothpicks, staples, film, toothpaste, toilet paper, tenpenny nails, stamps, an oil change, gas for the lawn mower, and food for the pets.

* Making a list compels you to *get organized:* You can think through your day, decide what's important, and give yourself some goals.

* Crossing off those errands, deadlines, reminders, and tasks gives you a *positive feeling of accomplishment*—a feel-good measuring stick.

* Even if you don't cross off all of the items, at least you know you've handled the most important ones and you can just add the rest onto tomorrow's list.

KEEP A SMALL NOTEPAD

Stick it in your back pocket, briefcase, or glove compartment, and have a pen close at hand. It's very easy to keep a running inventory of the things that occur to you but that you know will be forgotten about sixty seconds from now if you don't write them down. Sooner or later, list making will become a habit as the value of those lists becomes evident.

DON'T OVERDO LISTS

A list becomes self-defeating when you put too many action items on it. Your list can K2 you when it starts to look too damned daunting. Use it to prioritize tasks; get the most important of them done today, and carry the rest over to tomorrow. Unless something is a life-or-death matter or involves cash or a game, it can usually wait.

MANDATORY ADVICE
Always Keep Instruction Manuals

They come with everything you buy: large appliances for the kitchen and laundry; small electrics from coffeemakers to waffle irons; TVs, VCRs, DVDs, and other electronic components; grills, clocks, tools, and more.

1. First, read them. In addition to letting you know how to clean, maintain, and get the most enjoyment out of your purchases, these manuals always seem to reveal some neat feature or capability you would never know about otherwise. I recently bought a small TV/VCR combo for the kitchen and learned that it could automatically skip over all the commercials on a tape during playback. All I have to do is push a button or two and it's my dream come true: solid game, with no time between innings, quarters, or periods. If I hadn't been breezing through those trusty directions, I never would have known about it.

2. Second, put them all into *one file*. That way you'll instantly know where to find the one you need. Sooner or later, you *will* need it—when your shiatsu massager goes on the blink or you forget how to program your multiple-disk CD changer.

3. When filing, staple the receipt and warranty to the owner's manual. If you need to have the item repaired or return it, all the paperwork you need will be together.

EFFICIENT HOUSECLEANERS USE LISTS, TOO

In addition to helping you live the organized, low-hassle life most guys dream of, devising and following a list is the most effective way to clean house, too. Which makes this the ideal jumping-off point into the next chapter. . . .

HOUSECLEANING BATTLE PLAN

How to Attack a Room

Conventional wisdom says that the best way to get from point A to point B is to figure out all the little things you have to accomplish between the two. But with housecleaning, a major hurdle for men is having no idea where to begin. Too often we're stranded at point A, paralyzed with confusion.

The solution is pretty simple. A *housecleaning list* can help a man find the starting point in every room, and then move through domestic chores like a shark through chum. So we'll first talk about how to make and use a cleaning list. Then we'll move out of the classroom and into the house for a full-blown, room-by-room *Clean Like a Man* experience.

Just List It

Doing housework as quickly and painlessly as possible is *definitely* a matter of having a strategy, a system, a schedule, a routine . . . and a cleaning list is, really, all of these things. "To-do" lists usually include things you need to do every day, once a week, monthly, or even seasonally (although planning that far in advance may be pushing the organizational envelope for most guys). They're basically reminders that help you keep track of routine tasks and when they should be done.

With a system and a regular timetable, you can stay on top of housekeeping and keep it from getting out of hand. Dirty clothes and dishes don't pile up, clutter doesn't go unchecked, bedding doesn't get stale, dust and dirt don't overaccumulate to the point of overwhelming you. When these things build up—which happens all too easily in a man's world—things can quickly spin out of control.

Other strategic advantages of lists:

* With a clear plan of attack you're more focused, goal-oriented, and effective.
* You see what needs to be done and that your chores are finite.
* You never have to wonder what to do next.
* You maintain a regular schedule. When you stay on top of the easy stuff that takes just minutes, it doesn't turn into a monster: a huge, difficult, time-consuming chore. So you're always in position to get your house comfortably clean and tidy in minutes.
* You have goals. Tweak your competitive gene with a list. See how fast you can get everything on your bathroom list done; then next time, try to beat your "personal best" time. Or simply use your list as a motivational tool: Every "done" checkmark gets you closer to your finish line.

EASY AS ONE, TWO, THREE . . .

Just the act of jotting down your chores is an advantage. Like all lists, it will help you break the big job into a series of smaller tasks, prioritize them, organize your plan of attack, and achieve that wonderful glow of accomplishment as you check off one thing after another.

Here's an example of how you might break your weekly "clean the bathroom" routine down into manageable bites:

1. Clean sink.
2. Clean tub, shower.
3. Clean toilet.

4. Clean counter and mirror.
5. Clean floor.

Seeing these few chores written down lets you divide the seemingly large job of "cleaning the bathroom" into a series of easy little chores. And if all your supplies are right under the bathroom sink or in your MCU, each task will take only a few minutes. Let's use the kitchen to illustrate how a list can help you prioritize. Your list might include:

1. Clean sink, counters.
2. Clean stovetop.
3. Clean oven.
4. Sweep and damp-mop floor.
5. Clean refrigerator interior.
6. Dust refrigerator cooling coils.

With this list you can do the most important things first, and maybe even figure out which jobs have to be done only periodically. For example, you sure don't have to clean out the refrigerator every week, so it might move onto your *monthly* list. Dusting the fridge cooling coils has "semiannual" written all over it. And cleaning the oven might be on your "monthly" or "never" list, depending on your cooking habits (my own oven is as clean as the day I moved in: it's never been used). So the list becomes:

1. Clean sink, counters.
2. Clean stovetop.
3. ~~Clean oven.~~ *(it's not dirty)*
4. Sweep and damp-mop floor.
5. ~~Clean refrigerator interior.~~ *(do next week)*
6. ~~Dust refrigerator cooling coils.~~ *(do in June)*

Pretty cool how that works, isn't it?

SAMPLE CLEANING LISTS

The following sample lists focus on very routine "maintenance" housekeeping for the most important rooms. As you can see from the approximate times, the whole show takes just a matter of minutes each day.

Daily Cleaning List

TASK	TIME IT TAKES
Make the bed	2 minutes
After showering, squeegee walls and spritz with Tilex	2 minutes
Wipe out sinks after use	1 minute
Rinse dishes after meals and put in dishwasher	2 minutes
Wipe off kitchen counters	1 minute
Sweep hard-surface floors in high-traffic areas	2 minutes
Put away newspapers and clear away clutter	1 minute
Total time per day:	11 minutes*

*You probably don't have to sweep the floors or wipe off the kitchen counters *every* day. That cuts the time you spend on routine housekeeping chores to as little as eight minutes per day—pretty undemanding.

Try out the basic daily tactics for a while, then incorporate the weekly and monthly ones and you might be surprised at just how painless a cleaning routine can be.

THE IMPORTANCE OF PACE

I included the rough times for each task to help you put housecleaning in perspective and to set the stage for *blitzcleaning*, in which "timing is everything" (see Chapter 7). Blitzcleaning's goal is to accelerate the pace, which helps you focus on the task at hand, eliminate distractions, and finish a whole lot faster.

While the next set of lists doesn't include times for each chore, I guarantee that if you push yourself a little you'll be more focused and much more effective. What's more, each task will take a lot more time if you just putter along at your usual undisciplined pace, getting distracted every couple of minutes—petting the dog, taking a quick peek at your latest *Sports Illustrated*, grabbing some pretzels, seeing if that neighbor babe is washing her car, channel-surfing.

There are scores of distractions to sidetrack you, and a man will take advantage of every one of them to avoid housekeeping. So concentrate only on housecleaning, at least for a little while.

WEEKLY CLEANING LIST*

KITCHEN

* Take out the garbage (you probably will do this every two or three days as needed).
* Check the fridge for food decomposed to the point of inedibility; discard.
* Sweep and damp-mop the floors.

BATHROOM

* Windex the bathroom mirror.
* Clean the sink and countertop.
* Clean the toilet (may be necessary to do more than once a week).
* Sweep and damp-mop the floors.

BEDROOM

* Launder bed linens and towels.
* Dust visible surfaces.
* Remake the bed with fresh linens.
* Vacuum the carpets and rugs.

DINING AND LIVING ROOMS

* Dust visible surfaces.
* Vacuum the upholstery.
* Vacuum the carpets and rugs.

MONTHLY OR QUARTERLY CLEANING LIST

Work these jobs into your routine every few months.

KITCHEN

* Dust the refrigerator coils.
* Clean the refrigerator interior.

*Note: If your standards are not extremely rigid, you could get by doing most of these jobs once every ten days to two weeks.

BATHROOM

* Clean the grout between shower tiles.

BEDROOM

* Turn the mattress.
* Wash or air-freshen the pillows.

ALL ROOMS

* Do serious dusting (tops of door frames, appliances, cupboards, bookcases, ceiling fan blades, and other furniture above eye level).
* Wash the windows, windowblinds, and the picture glass.
* Clean under furniture and appliances.

SEASONAL OR OCCASIONAL CLEANING LIST

* Store clothing that's out of season.
* Clean and reorganize the closets.
* Clean the garage.
* Wash the window blinds.

A Clean Sweep

You're finally ready for your virtual housecleaning experience: a room-by-room walk-through that will show you how all the right cleaning tools, products, techniques, and strategies come into play—and how fast and easy housekeeping can be.

LIVING ROOM

Along with the bedroom and the den, this is considered a "dry room" as far as cleaning goes, because your use of liquid cleaning solutions, particularly water, is fairly limited. Cleaning dry rooms mostly involves dusting, vacuuming, sweeping, and damp-wiping. (Kitchens and bathrooms are "wet rooms" where liquid cleaners are used a lot; in addition, both have running water, faucets, sinks, and other plumbing fixtures.)

Let's concentrate on what might well be a typical guy's *living room*. A brief description: It's carpeted and has a sofa and several small but comfortable chairs surrounding a coffee table. There are windows on one or two of the walls, several doorways, a few lamps, a bookcase, and maybe a fireplace. It goes without saying that everything is extremely tasteful.

Most of the following procedures also apply to other dry rooms.

TOOLS AND SUPPLIES

In the room:

* Vacuum with extension hose(s), one or two rigid extension tubes, and nozzle attachments (dust brushes, crevice tool, upholstery tool, etc.)
* A wastebasket or a garbage bag

In your MCU (carryall kit):

* Dust wand (feather duster)
* Clean, dry cotton terry cloths or rags
* Cleaning solutions in spray bottles: Windex for glass and most other surfaces; an all-purpose cleaner like Fantastik, Formula 409, Orange Clean, or a solution of mild dish soap and water; Pledge or Endust; stain remover like OxiClean or Resolve (you don't need any sanitizing disinfectant spray—this is for "wet rooms" that provide a much better environment for germs)

On your person:

* Walkman (always)

PROCEDURE

Methodically work your way around the room. If you're right-handed, a clockwise direction probably works best. Lefties should go counterclockwise. You may have to circle the room several times as you work from high to low. Here's the basic progression:

1. *Unclutter.* Clear tables and floors; place debris in a wastebasket or a garbage bag.
2. *Dust.* As you go around the room for the first time, dust at all levels. Above eye level: Extend the handle of a dust wand (or use a vacuum with dust-brush attachments) and remove ceiling cobwebs; dust the tops of window and door frames; dust the top shelves of bookcases and ceiling fan blades. At eye level: Dust lamp shades and picture frames, then move down to the coffee table, the woodwork, and the remaining bookcase shelves (on these items you can use Pledge or Endust with cotton cloths).
3. *Clean glass and woodwork.* Go around the room again: Clean picture glass, mirrors, and windows with Windex and cotton cloths; damp-wipe light-switch plates, doorknobs, doors, and other woodwork with an all-purpose cleaner and cotton cloths.
4. *Vacuum.* Go around the room a final time: Vacuum baseboards with a utility brush; vacuum the sofa and the chairs with an upholstery attachment; vacuum the floor on your way out.

BEDROOM

This dry room is similar to the living room but there's one difference: Bedding goes into the laundry. This strategy can be viewed as a delay, but it really creates an opportunity (see "Downtime Cleanups," opposite).

TOOLS AND SUPPLIES

Assemble the same gear you used to clean the living room.

PROCEDURE

1. *Strip the bed.* Place sheets, pillowcases, and other washables into a bag or a hamper; launder them.
2. *Unclutter.* Store clothing; throw away debris.
3. *Dust.* Work your way around the room. Start high and work

down, using a dust wand or vacuum. Above eye level: Remove ceiling cobwebs; dust the tops of window and door frames, ceiling fan blades, etc. At eye level: Dust lamp shades, picture frames, and headboard. Dust the remaining woodwork and the furniture using Pledge and Endust and cotton cloths.

4. *Clean glass and woodwork.* Go around the room again: Clean picture glass, mirrors, and windows with Windex and cotton cloths; damp-wipe light-switch plates, doorknobs, doors, and other woodwork with an all-purpose cleaner and cotton cloths; spot-clean smudges on walls with an all-purpose cleaner.

5. *Vacuum.* Go around a final time: Vacuum along baseboards; empty wastebaskets; vacuum the floor on your way out.

KITCHEN

TOOLS AND SUPPLIES

In the room:

* Vacuum with extension hose(s), one or two rigid extension tubes, and nozzle attachments
* Sponge mop, Swiffer, or ReadyMop
* Bucket, preferably with two compartments
* Broom and dustpan

In your MCU:

* Dust wand (feather duster)

HOME **MAN**AGEMENT TIP
Someday You Won't Need a List

After a few cleaning run-throughs in each room, you'll tweak my sample lists and devise your own customized versions. Your personal system of cleaning will evolve; your need for a list will diminish. Then your muscle memory will take over. You'll instinctively know what and how to clean because your personal "system" will be ingrained into your manly being.

* Clean, dry cotton terry cloths or rags
* Medium/large sponge
* Small Scotch-Brite sponge
* Cleaning solutions in spray bottles: Windex for glass and most other surfaces; an all-purpose cleaner; a disinfectant like Lysol or Pine-Sol Antibacterial Spray for sanitizing

On your person:

* Walkman
* Rubber gloves (optional)

PROCEDURE

1. *Unclutter.* Clear counters and consolidate items while cleaning.
2. *Prep-clean surfaces.* Spray all-purpose cleaner on any tough spots, old spills, or dried-on food you see on the counters and range top; let it soak. If you need to, remove the drip pans from underneath the stove burners and soak them in hot, soapy water.
3. Go around the room and do the following: *dust* high spots like the tops of appliances, cupboards, doors, and window frames; *spritz* and wipe down appliances, stovetop, counters, cabinets, tables, and chairs with Windex or an all-purpose cleaner and a sponge, then dry off with cotton cloths; clean the inside of the microwave with an all-purpose cleaner and a sponge.

4. *Backtrack.* If necessary, scrub soaking drip pans with a Scotch-Brite sponge; then rinse, dry, and replace on the stove. Clean the garbage disposal gasket with an old toothbrush and baking soda or an all-purpose cleaner; put ice cubes into the garbage disposal and turn it on while running cold water (this cleans the blades). Check the refrigerator for post-peak food; discard. Clean, scrub, and sanitize the sink with Lysol and a Scotch-Brite sponge. Polish the sink faucet fixtures.

5. *Sweep or vacuum-dust* the floor. Remove the trash. Swiffer, ReadyMop, or wash the floor on your way out.

6. *If needed:* Wash the windows and the walls; vacuum the blinds; clean the oven; clean the refrigerator interior.

BATHROOM

TOOLS AND SUPPLIES

* Everything you used in the kitchen, plus a shower, tub, and tile cleaner, Lime-A-Way, toilet bowl cleaner, toilet brush
* Rubber gloves (bathroom chemicals are a little stronger, so protect your hands)

PROCEDURE

1. *Shake the rugs.* Then put them outside the bathroom.
2. *Clean the toilet.* Flush, add cleaner/sanitizer, and let it sit.
3. *Dust.* Use a dust wand or a vacuum attachment above eye level: window and door ledges, top of mirror, and light fixtures.
4. *Clean glass.* Use Windex on the mirror, damp-wipe light fixtures with a cotton cloth.
5. *Wipe the sink.* Wipe stray hairs up with toilet paper.
6. *Clean the counters, sink, and fixtures.* Spritz with Windex or Lysol to sanitize; wipe with a sponge; dry with a cotton cloth.
7. *Clean the shower and the tub.* Apply tub and tile cleaner and Lime-A-Way (if needed). Rinse with water and wipe dry with a cotton cloth or a squeegee.
8. *Finish cleaning the toilet* with a toilet brush. Flush.
9. *Clean the floor.* Sweep and damp-mop.
10. *If needed:* Wash windows and walls; vacuum blinds.

You're done! And there's still time to play eighteen!

7

BLITZCLEANING
How to "Vroom-Vroom" Through a Room

litzcleaning is an exclusive *Clean Like a Man* concept: an original and very effective approach to housekeeping. The secret is simply working at breakneck speed. Here's how:

BE PREPARED
Gather all supplies (vacuum, spray solutions, sponges and rags, etc.) and place them in your MCU or wherever you can get to them quickly.

SET A TIME LIMIT
This is probably the most effective blitzcleaning strategy. Set a stovetop timer for fifteen minutes and try to accomplish as much as you can before the bell. Make housecleaning a game. Put yourself on a clock every time you clean, and log how long it takes to finish each room. Then try to beat your record.

WORK FROM A LIST
Written objectives give you goals and remove indecision.

Ten-Minute Crisis Cleanup

The phone rings, and someone has decided to drop in unexpectedly. It could be the best of times (the babe you met at a party last Saturday night) or the worst of times (your mother-in-law or a roving band of unwanted relatives). Either way, you have to clean up fast, because the place looks like a scene out of *Animal House*. Here's a solution that's designed purely for speed, not style:

1. Grab a large box or a bag and head first to the entryway, then to the area(s) in which you and your guests are likely to spend the most time. Throw everything that doesn't belong in that area into your box. Hide the filled box in a room or closet you know won't be used. Close the doors to any messy rooms.
2. Grab your MCU containing Windex, cotton cloths, dusting/furniture polish spray, sponges, whisk broom, etc., plus your vacuum cleaner, and make the most of the rest of your time.
3. Head for the living room. Grab a cotton cloth and whip the most visible dust off tabletops. Straighten magazines into neat stacks and arrange sofa pillows. Spritz a little Lemon Pledge into the room (it has a nice aroma that says "this room is clean").

FOCUS
Work without distractions—no phone, TV, other people, etc. Concentrate only on what's in front of you.

LISTEN TO MUSIC
Music is the only allowable diversion. High-energy music is recommended. Dancing, however, is strictly forbidden.

CIRCLE THE ROOM
Start at one point in the room and methodically work your way around it in one direction, cleaning what's right in front of you as you go.

KEEP MOVING
The faster the better. Don't think, just stay in perpetual motion.

4. Head for the bathroom most likely to be used. Grab the Windex or the lemon-scented Lysol and a sponge or cotton cloth from under the sink. Wipe stray hairs out of the sink with toilet paper, then spray it and give it a quick once-over with the cloth or the sponge. Dry with the cloth. Spray and wipe down the toilet, too. Spray Lysol into the tub or the shower enclosure (the whole room will smell clean). Whip all clutter into the vanity below the sink.

5. Head for the kitchen. If there are dishes in the sink, throw them into the dishwasher. If you have no dishwasher, put dishes and any other clutter into a plastic tub and hide it in the oven, a closet, or the garage. Spray the countertops and/or the table with Windex and wipe off. Take out the garbage if time allows.

6. Turn the lights down low or draw the drapes to diminish visibility (this is also called "light cleaning").

7. Buy yourself some extra time when you first receive that call by using preplanned excuses: "I just got out of the shower . . . give me about a half hour to get squared away," or "I'm on the other line with my [doctor, spiritual adviser, mother, boss, parole officer]. Let me call you the minute we're finished."

8. Finally, remember that the first thing your guests will see when you open the door is you, so make sure you're fully clothed.

DON'T WASTE A MOMENT

Multitask at every opportunity. If you have a load of laundry going, straighten up the containers on the laundry-room shelves—or try to organize the whole room before the final rinse.

DON'T WASTE A MOTION

If you're going upstairs, grab something that belongs up there and take it along. You might even put it away once you arrive.

DON'T BE A PERFECTIONIST

If it's not dirty, skip it. Or just spot-clean. Surface cleaning will be perfectly fine—and it's *always* better than nothing.

part two

GAME TIME

{Going Room to Room}

Here's where you move out of the class-room and into a dirty house, building on what you learned in Part I with manly helpings of room-specific information.

THE FRONT BURNER
Kitchen Cleanups

Whether you live in an apartment or a mansion, the kitchen is probably the most popular, most frequented, hardest-working area in the house. It's the place where people congregate at big parties and intimate, casual get-togethers alike. It's the comfort food of rooms.

Your kitchen has it all, cleaning-wise: plumbing, large and small appliances, a floor, light fixtures, counters and shelves, cabinets and cupboards, wood, metal, tile, porcelain. It certainly contains the most items to be maintained on a regular basis. It's also the place where you keep food—much of which is perishable and can harbor microbes that are very capable of taking you down if you don't handle and store your groceries wisely. All of this adds up to the most potential for clutter, messes, and mechanical snafus, plus the most daunting challenges for ongoing maintenance and cleaning. But you, sir, will easily handle it when you *Clean Like a Man!*

Countertops

Kitchen countertops really take a beating, what with knives slicing across them, hot pots and pans sitting on them, and all kinds of food and drink spilling on them. It's no surprise, since countertops are the areas where all your food preparation takes place. For you, "food prep" might mean unwrapping a frozen pizza or unscrewing a jar of jalapeño cheese dip. But still, your countertops should be sanitary, and they should be kept clean and clear of debris, stains, and clutter to keep that Food Network look going. Here are some guidelines:

* Use cutting boards as much as possible. They protect countertops from cuts and stains.
* If you do spill something, clean it up immediately with an all-purpose cleaner and a sponge, a cotton cloth, or a paper towel. Left untended, many spills can stain or otherwise damage your surfaces.
* If you have a stubborn stain, try mixing up a paste consisting of about 1 tablespoon each of water and baking soda, apply it to the stain, and let it work for a while before wiping and rinsing.
* Don't put hot cookware directly on countertops. You can get some nice tiles down at Home Depot for about a buck apiece, and they make very manly trivets.

Large Appliances

GARBAGE DISPOSAL

TOP TIPS

* Keep the disposal clear by running cold water *before, during, and after* you dispose of garbage. Running water for thirty to sixty seconds after you turn off the disposal flushes the remaining food particles all the way down the drain and keeps it clear.
* Use tongs, *not* your hand, to reach in and remove foreign objects.
* Things *not* to put in the garbage disposal: metal, rubber, glass, or plastic; banana peels, rhubarb, corn husks, or other fibrous, stringy foods; potato peels; fruit pits and other hard items; liquefied fats; cleaning solutions except those made especially for disposals, such as Disposer Care.

HOME **MAN**AGEMENT TIP
How to Streamline Kitchen Cleanups

Keeping up with just a few low-hassle tasks will help you stay out in front of cleaning the kitchen (and will make it look better, too).

* Minimize clutter on countertops, windowsills, appliances, etc.
* Store small appliances out of sight if you don't use them daily.
* Stash as much as possible of everything (spices, cookbooks, dishes, etc.) in cupboards.
* Put dirty dishes into the dishwasher after *every* meal.
* If you don't have a dishwasher, either get one or move.
* Try to be fanatical about keeping the sink and the counters free of dried-on spatters and spills—in other words, as sparkling clean as possible.
* Do away with all the decorative crap you can.
* Keep the refrigerator clear of objets d'art, magnetized and otherwise.

* Consult your instruction manual if your garbage disposal becomes clogged, runs but doesn't grind, makes loud whirring noises, is dripping from the bottom, or drains very slowly or stops completely. (Your owner's manual should be in that big file dedicated to manuals.)

CLEANING

* To keep blades clean and break up grease on the rotors: toss in ice cubes, turn on the disposal, and run cold water.
* To keep odor free, put $1/2$ cup baking soda into a sink half-filled with warm water, remove the stopper, and let it drain through the running disposal. You can also add $1/2$ cup baking soda and $1/2$ cup white vinegar, wait a few minutes, and pour in a kettle of boiling water. Or grind up some orange, lemon, or lime peels and run them through.

MANDATORY ADVICE Manual Labor–Saver

This suggestion applies to *all* kitchen appliances and nearly everything else you purchase: Read the instruction manual cover to cover, then staple the store receipt and warranty onto it and keep it in an A-to-Z accordion file devoted to owner's manuals. Don't underestimate the value of this advice. When owner's manuals and receipts are all in one place, you can always find the one you need for troubleshooting advice.

＊ Clean the top and especially the underside of the rubber gasket covering the drain. Use baking soda on the scrubbing side of a damp Scotch-Brite sponge.

＊ Flush the whole system about twice a month: Place a stopper in the sink, fill the sink half full of cold water, remove the stopper, and turn on the disposal as the water runs through.

DISHWASHER

FAST FACTS

＊ Dishwashers use very hot water—140° to 160°F.—to clean and sanitize dishes. Some plastic items might melt.

＊ Never use regular liquid dishwashing detergent—you'll have suds all over the kitchen! Use only detergent made specifically for automatic dishwashers, even just to clean the interior.

＊ The dishwasher door needs to be latched shut or it won't operate.

＊ Dishwashers usually drain into the kitchen sink drainpipe or through the garbage disposal.

＊ The newer your dishwasher, the less detergent you have to use. The latest models are so efficient that filling only about one-quarter to one-third of the detergent compartment's capacity with soap will probably do a fine job. It might take a little experimentation to find the ideal amount of detergent to use. See how your dishes turn out and adjust from there.

* Things *not* to put in your dishwasher: wooden spoons, wooden salad dishes, wooden cutting boards, or other wooden items; kitchen knives, especially if they're upscale ones; plastic tumblers (they will crack) or lightweight plastic containers (they might melt). Tupperware is okay, though.

If dishes are not getting 100 percent clean:

* Water may not be hot enough. Check your water heater and adjust its temperature setting if needed.
* Scrape and rinse food residue off your dishes more thoroughly before putting them into the dishwasher.
* Use a little more detergent.
* Load fewer dishes more loosely in the main compartment. Overloading may block the water spray that cleans dishes or jam the dishwasher's rotating spray arm.
* Make sure the detergent dispenser is opening during the wash cycle. If you think it isn't, take a look at it after the full washing cycle. Still closed? There may be hardened detergent or mineral deposits jamming it (if so, remove them), or perhaps your dispenser's electrical solenoid needs replacing (check your instruction manual).

If the unit is not draining, not filling with water, or not operating properly in any other way, *consult your instruction manual.* If you still can't fix the problem, *call a plumber.*

STRATEGIC **MAN**EUVER
With Plumbing, Being Macho May Not Be Smart

Some emergencies with the sink, the garbage disposal, and the dishwasher require the talents of a professional. It's not at all unmanly to call a plumber if you can't fix the problem yourself with help from the instruction manual.

CLEANING

* Clean the exterior with a clean, damp sponge, or spritz with a vinegar-and-water solution (about 1/4 cup vinegar to 1 pint water) and wipe off.
* Don't use abrasive cleaners on the dishwasher's interior or exterior.
* Clean occasionally around the door's rubber gasket seal—bits of food can sometimes stick there.
* If there's an unpleasant odor inside, toss 1/2 cup baking soda onto the bottom of the dishwasher and leave it.

REFRIGERATOR

For some reason, this appliance is a magnet for, well . . . magnets. Try to avoid the temptation to stick all sorts of elementary-school "art," lists, invitations, snapshots, announcements, and other assorted paperwork to the front or side of your fridge. It only adds to visual clutter and affects the whole kitchen.

CLEANING THE EXTERIOR

* About as no-muss, no-fuss as it gets. Just use a sponge with a little soapy water, or spritz it down with an all-purpose cleaner and wipe off with a sponge or a cotton cloth.
* Occasionally clean the rubber gasket that seals the door shut with warm, soapy water. Coating it with mineral oil will keep it from cracking.
* Remember, if you have a lot of junk stuck to the fridge, you'll have to clean around it.

CLEANING THE INTERIOR

* Discard spoiled food. Then put other foods aside and remove all the shelves and drawers you can.
* Don't use an all-purpose cleaner or anything with ammonia or alcohol in it; over time, this may dry out the plastic and cause cracking. Instead, mix 1 quart warm water with a handful of baking soda, wipe down the interior, then dry with a cotton cloth. The baking soda helps to remove odors, too.

HOME **MAN**AGEMENT TIPS
Focusing on the Fridge

* Don't overload the refrigerator with too many food items: This discourages cleaning because emptying its shelves and drawers makes the job too much of an inconvenience. Guys need it to be as convenient as possible to have any chance of cleaning. An overcrowded fridge also limits circulation of cooling air.

* Throw away aging condiments regularly. If you don't eat them within a year or two of purchase, you probably never will.

* To keep odors at bay, spread a generous amount of baking soda, ground coffee (new or used), or activated charcoal in a shallow bowl and place on a shelf.

* If your condenser coils are mounted in the back, pull your refrigerator a few inches from the wall to leave a little extra room for air to circulate around the coils. They'll cool more efficiently that way.

* Swab out the drawers (especially if you store meats in any of them) with a soap-and-water solution.

* My owner's manual recommends cleaning the interior and its compartments once a month or more often for safe food storage. Fat chance this will happen with a guy's refrigerator. But you should make an effort to keep at least the meat drawers clean and sanitary.

* Spot-clean spills as they happen to avoid extra toil when doing an overall cleaning.

CLEANING THE FREEZER

* Most late-model freezers are "frost-free." To clean, simply turn off the freezer using the little dials you'll find inside the refrigerator. Then wipe out the interior with a solution of a small amount of baking soda mixed with water (1 teaspoon baking

soda to 1 cup water), rinse with plain water and a sponge, turn back on, and replace the food items.

✻ If you happen to have an older model that still gets a frost buildup inside: place frozen items in a cooler, turn the freezer control knob to "off," keep the door open, and let it defrost. (To accelerate defrosting, place a pan of hot water into the freezer or use a hair dryer.) Then clean as described above.

CLEANING THE CONDENSER COILS

✻ These carry the Freon that pumps through your refrigerator and keeps everything cool. Condenser coils collect dust, which diminishes their effectiveness. They should be cleaned at least twice a year to keep them condensing efficiently.

✻ If the coils are located underneath your fridge, they're probably behind a plastic kick plate that's attached with spring clips. Just snap it off to get to the coils. It might be a tight fit, so use your vacuum's crevice tool, a yardstick wrapped with a sock, or a thin, long-handled bottle brush. Your car's snowbrush will work in a pinch.

✻ If the coils are in the back, roll the refrigerator out until you can easily reach and clean them.

✻ Note: Be gentle when cleaning to avoid damaging the coils: they can be fragile. If possible, unplug the fridge first to avoid any chance of shock.

SINK

Avoiding clogs before they occur isn't "drain surgery." Here are a few suggestions:

✻ Try to minimize the cooking grease and fats you rinse down the drain.

✻ Wipe greasy pans with a paper towel before washing them in the sink, or before rinsing them in the sink prior to putting them in the dishwasher.

✻ Clear kitchen drains every few weeks by pouring in $1/2$ cup baking soda and $1/2$ cup white vinegar, waiting for a few minutes while it bubbles, then pouring in a kettle of boiling water.

✻ You can also simply pour a pot of boiling water into the drain every couple of weeks, which helps to remove grease buildup and other debris.

CLEANING

PORCELAIN SINKS

* Try to avoid harsh abrasive cleaners like Comet. Instead, try spraying the sink surfaces with your all-purpose cleaner, letting it work, and sponging it off.
* If it's still a bit dingy, put baking soda or Bar Keepers Friend on a damp, Teflon-faced sponge, scrub, and rinse with plain water.
* If stains persist, fill the sink with a solution of 3 tablespoons bleach per gallon water; let it stand for an hour, drain, and rinse with plain water.

STAINLESS-STEEL SINKS

* No abrasive cleaners, no steel wool. They'll scratch the surface for sure.
* Spray on Windex or your all-purpose cleaner, or apply some warm, sudsy water, sponge it clean, and rinse with plain water.

FAUCETS

* Use Windex or your all-purpose cleaner, then sponge off and dry-polish with a cotton cloth or a paper towel.
* If there are lime or other mineral deposits, apply Lime-A-Way or a 50-50 solution of water and white vinegar, let sit, scrub with a Teflon sponge, and rinse with plain water.

CLEARING CLOGS

* Use a plunger first. Run enough water so the drain opening is submerged, then place the plunger's rubber suction cup over the drain opening. (You might have to cover the garbage disposal opening, or a second drain in a double sink, to seal the connection and ensure suction.) Now give it ten or twenty vigorous pumps. Try this two or three times. You'll either push or pull the clog loose, or not.
* Next, try to clear the drain with baking soda and vinegar (see

MANDATORY ADVICE
Be Careful with Chemical Drain Openers!

When you use chemicals to open a clogged drain, you could be letting a genie out of the bottle. Follow these precautions:

* Read labels and make sure you're using the right stuff for the clog you're trying to beat. Alkalies are the remedy for grease buildup. Acids dissolve debris like soap scum, hair, and bits of food residue.
* *Don't mix alkalies with acids—they could explode!* In fact, don't mix any two chemical cleaning solutions together. *Ever.*
* Don't lean over and look down the drain after you've poured in any chemical—it could boil up and damage your eyes or sinuses.
* Never use chemical solvents in your garbage disposal.

page 104), or use a chemical solution like Drano (see "Be Careful with Chemical Drain Openers!" above, for precautions).

* If your drain is still blocked, use a large wrench to carefully remove the P-trap section of pipe below the sink (have a pail underneath to catch water and any gunk that might be in there). If you find the blockage here, at the lowest point, just clean it out and replace the pipe.
* No luck yet? Then the clog is still farther down the drain line. With the P-trap off, run a plumber's snake (you can rent one wherever you rent other serious tools, or buy one at a hardware store) through the drainpipe to dislodge the blockage.
* If all this fails, check other drains in your home. If more than one of them is stopped up, something is probably jammed in your "main drain"—the large underground pipe that leads out of your home and into the city sewer. At this point you can either get a plumbing how-to book or call Roto-Rooter. I strongly suggest the latter.

MICROWAVE

Taking care of the microwave may be as close as a guy can get to a no-brainer in the kitchen. There's probably not much reason to ever sanitize it, since every time you turn it on, any microbes inside are nuked into vapor.

CLEANING

* Simply take a damp sponge or a cotton cloth and wipe down the interior as soon as you see that something has spilled or bubbled over.
* To remove dried-on foods, boil a small bowl of water in the microwave, wait a few minutes while the steam works on the stain, then wipe it up.
* Don't use any abrasive cleaners or pads on microwave surfaces. You'll probably never have to anyway.
* To clean the front, just spray with Windex and wipe, or use a coffee filter dampened with soapy water.

RANGE AND STOVE

With so many different models in use today, specific advice isn't all that practical. Give your owner's manual a quick read-through and note the following cleaning instructions.

CLEANING KNOBS

* Pull them off and soak them in soapy dishwater. After they've soaked, clean off stubborn grease or residue with an old toothbrush.
* While they're soaking, clean the surfaces underneath the knobs as well as the rest of the stovetop with an all-purpose cleaner. Spray it on and let it work for a while, then sponge off. Don't use abrasive cleaners.

CLEANING DRIP PANS

* If you have a gas stove, remove the metal grate on top of each burner and lift off the drip pan that's underneath. If your stove is electric, the burners probably tilt upward (or else they unplug

and lift completely off the stove), allowing you to remove the drip pans.

* You can run drip pans through a dishwasher cycle or soak them in hot soapy water, then scrub. They can be scrubbed much harder than the stovetop can.

CLEANING THE STOVETOP

* Chances are your stovetop has a baked-on enamel finish. But regardless of its finish, don't use harsh abrasive cleaners or pads—they'll scratch.
* For regular cleaning, use soapy water and a sponge or a cotton cloth. For cleaning up grease, use a degreasing cleaner like Formula 409, Fantastik, or Orange Clean.
* If you need a stronger cleanser, first mix about 1 tablespoon baking soda (the kindest scouring powder of all) with enough water to make a paste and give it a try. If that isn't effective enough, move up to a mild liquid scouring cleanser like Soft Scrub, or a dry one like Bar Keepers Friend applied on a damp sponge. Then sponge off the residue with clear water.
* If you have a tough, baked-on spot of food, dribble a little water on it and let it soften up before wiping away. Rinse off the residue with water and a sponge.
* The best time to clean the stovetop is after a messy meal prep when the stove is still slightly warm. Don't give foods time to dry and cake onto the stove's surface.

OVEN

A friend of mine always hides his wife's Christmas gifts in the oven because he knows she never uses it. If you're the same way and have a small kitchen to boot, use the oven as storage space for extra cookware, small appliances you seldom need, or even snack crackers or other foods. If you actually use your oven for cooking, however, you'll have to clean it occasionally.

There are three kinds of ovens: conventional, self-cleaning, and continuous-cleaning. Unfortunately, even the two ovens with "cleaning" in their name will require periodic cleaning by you. There are so many different oven brands and models that only the most general advice will be offered here. Most experts advise that you do not use chemical oven cleaners on self-cleaning or continuous-cleaning ovens. Consult your owner's manual before cleaning *whatever* kind of unit you have.

CLEANING A CONVENTIONAL OVEN

✳ Use one of the "fumeless" cleaners that are now available. Leave the cleaner on the oven's interior surface for *at least* as long as the product instructions tell you to. This gives it more of a chance to work on grease and baked-on food residue. Then wipe it off with a sponge or paper towels and repeat if necessary.

✳ Option two: Make baking soda–water paste, apply it to the oven walls and floor, leave overnight, then redampen and scrub with a plastic scrubber. Rinse with plain water.

✳ Another approach: Put 1/2 cup ammonia into a bowl, place into the oven, and close the door. Let it work on grease and residue overnight, then wipe the interior out with paper towels. Don't turn the oven on during this process—and extinguish the pilot light if you have a gas oven.

CLEANING OVEN RACKS

✳ Put them into your bathtub or laundry-room sink, run hot water over them, add 1 cup automatic dishwasher detergent, and soak them until they're clean. If scrubbing's still needed, use a Scotch-Brite sponge.

CLEANING THE BROILER PAN

✳ Before each use, line the pan with foil to catch grease drips.
✳ If needed, clean ASAP after broiling to prevent grease and residue from hardening on its surface.
✳ Soak the tray insert (the part with perforated holes) in hot water mixed with 1/2 cup automatic dishwasher detergent until the gunk loosens up, then sponge it away or scrub with a Scotch-Brite sponge.

CLEANING A SELF-CLEANING OVEN

✳ These use very high temperatures to clean the oven's interior. After a self-cleaning cycle (about three to four hours), all you have to do is wipe out a little ashy residue.

STRATEGIC **MAN**EUVER
How to Avoid Oven Cleaning

* Don't use the oven. Or . . .
* If you're baking a pizza or anything else (casserole, pie, cobbler, etc.) that might drip onto the oven floor, place a cookie sheet or a piece of foil onto the rack just below it. Drippings will fall onto it and you'll avoid major oven cleanings longer. (But your foil or cookie sheet shouldn't cover an entire rack—it might block heat distribution and throw off your cooking time.)
* If food does happen to get onto the bottom or sides of the oven, try to clean it up right away, before it bakes on.

* Scrub the parts of the oven that aren't affected by the self-cleaning heat, like the edges just outside and inside of the rubber gasket that seals in the heat. Clean these extra parts *before* the self-cleaning process starts. Use hot, soapy water or, for tougher stains, a baking soda–water paste. *Don't* clean the gasket itself, or it will become prone to cracking and deterioration.
* Remove the oven racks and the broiler pan (and Christmas presents!) before starting the self-cleaning cycle. Clean them by hand, or follow the instructions above.
* Pull the knobs and the dials off before starting the self-cleaning process. The extremely high heat tends to weaken connectors on knobs and dials, and when those plastic pieces crack or break, replacing them is very pricey.
* Don't use chemical oven cleaners in a self-cleaning oven.
* And read your instruction manual carefully!

CLEANING A CONTINUOUS-CLEANING OVEN

The interior surface is porous, so it's more resistant to stains and absorbs grease better than standard or self-cleaning ovens. Even so, it will need occasional cleaning.

* First remove the oven racks and the broiler pan; clean according to the instructions for a self-cleaning oven.
* To clean the interior, just wipe out with a Scotch-Brite sponge and plain water.
* Clean up large spills or boil-overs while the oven is still warm, using a sponge with water or paper towels. Blot, don't rub, to avoid clogging the oven's porous surface with gunk.
* You can use all-purpose cleaners and rub gently with a Scotch-Brite sponge, but be sure to rinse the cleaned areas with plain water.
* Don't use chemical oven cleaners! Read the instruction manual!

RANGE HOOD

If you have one, its fan will either be vented to the outside or contain a replaceable charcoal filter designed to remove greasy vapors, steam, smoke, and cooking smells.

CLEANING

* Wipe down the exterior with a solution of several drops of grease-cutting dishwashing liquid mixed with hot water. Add a little ammonia if the going is really greasy.
* Charcoal filters need to be replaced at least once a year—more often if you cook a lot, less often if you don't.
* Clean mesh filters with a 3:1 water-ammonia solution.
* Check your instruction manual for specifics.
* Just sponge off the fan blades and cover with warm water mixed with grease-cutting dishwashing liquid or a water-ammonia solution. (Use rubber gloves.)

Small Appliances and Tools

BLENDER

CLEANING

Either run it through the dishwasher or make it a "self-cleaning" appliance: Fill the blender halfway with warm water, put in a drop or two of dishwashing liquid, and run on high for ten seconds.

COFFEE GRINDER

Coffee beans contain oils that can get rancid and cause a bitter flavor in brewed coffee. Keep your grinder clean and free of ground-coffee residue to help prevent this.

CLEANING

* Wipe out ground coffee residue after each use with a paper towel or a damp sponge.
* Rinse the top with water and a little dishwashing detergent, then dry.

COFFEEMAKER

According to *Consumer Reports*, the key to making great coffee is a squeaky-clean pot. My mother always claimed it was using good, cold water. Still others swear that high-grade coffee is the secret. But why take chances? It's not so tough to apply all three tricks, and any others you may pick up on the street.

CLEANING

* Clean all washable parts with detergent and warm water to remove the coffee residue that can cause bitter coffee.

STRATEGIC **MAN**EUVER
Multitasking Coffee Filters

* Painting up high? Poke your brush through the middle of a coffee filter and it will catch paint drips.
* Use lint-free filters to wipe down your microwave window, TV and computer screens, binoculars, eyeglasses, and other surfaces for which using Windex or other chemicals isn't recommended.
* If wine has tiny bits of cork in it, strain it through a coffee filter.
* Cover foods cooking in the microwave with a coffee filter to prevent spattering.

✳ Run white vinegar through the system every month or so to keep the coffeemaker free of mineral deposits. With all filters in place, pour about three-quarters of a carafe of vinegar or a vinegar-water solution into the reservoir. Start the unit, run half of the vinegar through, then shut off the coffeemaker for fifteen to thirty minutes. Turn the coffeemaker back on and run the rest through. Pour the same vinegar in again and run it through once more. Then pour in a full carafe of fresh water and run it through to clear out the vinegar residue. You can put the used vinegar into a specially marked container and reuse it for coffeemaker cleaning. It's good for four or five run-throughs. Ultimately, you can pour it down drains or into the garbage disposal to keep them fresh.

WOODEN CUTTING BOARD

Apply mineral oil occasionally to keep the wood conditioned. Don't use vegetable or olive oil: They can get rancid. Wood can absorb soap, so use soap only to clean plastic cutting boards.

CLEANING

✳ Use a mixture of 3 tablespoons bleach to 1 gallon water (less than 1 tablespoon per quart—it doesn't take much). Wipe off the cutting board with this solution and a Scotch-Brite sponge, then rinse well and dry.

NONSTICK-COATED PANS (TEFLON)

Do not use a metal spatula or other metal utensils when cooking in these pans, or steel wool when cleaning them. Metal will scratch the finish and diminish the nonstick effectiveness.

CLEANING

✳ Scrub with hot, soapy water and a Scotch-Brite sponge, or run them through the dishwasher.

PLASTIC CONTAINERS

This category includes Rubbermaid, Tupperware, Ziploc, and other brands. Some foods, particularly tomato sauce and carrots, can stain them pretty noticeably.

CLEANING

* First, try soaking in hot water with dishwashing detergent.
* If that fails to remove stains, move to stage 2: Soak in a solution of 1 tablespoon chlorine bleach in 1 cup water (don't add detergent to this mixture).
* You can also try that old faithful paste of baking soda and water.
* To stop stains before they start, rinse containers after every use in cold water, then wash in warm, soapy water right away.

TOASTER OVEN

CLEANING

The smartest toaster-oven cleaning you can do is right after spatters and boil-overs occur, before they become baked on and tougher to remove.

* Make a habit of washing the rack, the crumb tray, the broiler pan, and even the glass door in the dishwasher as often as possible.
* Otherwise, clean the rack, the oven tray, and inside the glass door with a Scotch-Brite pad and soapy water, then rinse with clear water.
* Don't use all-purpose cleaners, spray-on glass cleaners, or abrasive cleansers like Comet.
* Wipe the exterior clean with a damp sponge or a cotton cloth.

TOASTER

* This is one of those appliances that can easily be stored in a cupboard if you don't use it frequently.
* Always unplug the unit and let it cool off before cleaning it.
* Never poke a fork or a knife into the toaster to dislodge a piece of toast that's stuck. You could damage the wirelike heating elements or get an electric shock. Instead, unplug the toaster, let it cool, turn it upside down, and shake it out.

CLEANING

* Unplug the toaster, make sure it's cool, and empty the crumb tray over the sink or a wastebasket.

* Spray a little window cleaner onto a cloth and wipe chrome toasters clean.
* Sponge off plastic toasters with soapy water. The ammonia in window cleaner tends to dry out and crack the plastic.

Storage

Try to store all the appliances and utensils you don't use every day out of sight. There's no reason to have them cluttering up your counters. You can get a lot of storage ideas by scanning the many ingenious products available at home stores or housewares departments. But measure all potential storage spaces before you go to the store—width, height, and depth—to save a lot of running back and forth.

Store items you use often in places where they're always easily accessible:

* Hang coffee mugs underneath a cupboard on small hooks.
* Mount the microwave above the stove, or place it on a rack so that it's off the countertop and store another appliance or cookbooks below it.
* Keep knives in their own standup block or in a magnetic holder hung on the wall.
* Store dishes in a cupboard above or near the dishwasher and silverware in an adjacent drawer.

When you store kitchen items in cupboards or cabinets, place the least-used appliances (fondue pot, Cuisinart, etc.) in back and keep the more frequently used ones up front. Likewise, stash your most-used dishes, glassware, and utensils at or just below eye level so they're easy to reach.

Next: Cooking Lessons?

Now you should know enough to keep your kitchen clean, well-organized, and running smoothly. Next, you might want to get a few cookbooks so you can expand your culinary horizons to include more than chips, dip, and frozen pizza.

GROOM WITH A VIEW

Bathroom Basics

The bathroom is arguably every man's favorite room. It's the comfortable haven where we go to shower, groom, read the sports page, sip coffee, set goals for the day ahead or reminisce about the day just completed, seek solitude, and find serenity. And it's a lot nicer when it's clean.

I've always enjoyed cleaning the bathroom because most of its surfaces are tile, porcelain, chrome, or glass—all waterproof. You can spray and slosh your cleaning liquids with reckless abandon, then just wipe them up with rags or towels. When you're done, everything *literally* sparkles and shines—"just like on TV." Best of all, cleaning and disinfecting the bathroom is not at all difficult or time-consuming when you *Clean Like a Man*.

Why Is a Clean Bathroom Important?

Besides the fact that you'll be spending time in the bathroom every day and you deserve a nice venue, there are two reasons to keep it clean: (1) the guests who are welcome and (2) the guests who aren't. The desirable guests are, of course, the female kind. The route to your bedroom will likely go through your bathroom first. If it's not clean, uncluttered, and inviting, it will probably become her last stop before she leaves. Even "just friends" females or casual visitors will eventually have to use your facilities. And for women, there are certain minimum requirements:

❋ The sink and the area surrounding it must be sparkling clean.

❋ The shower walls and curtain must be mildew-free and fresh smelling; the tub should be ring-free.

❋ There should be clean cotton towels near the sink and shower.

❋ There should be a relatively new bar of soap in a dish that's not caked with soap scum. A clear glycerin soap like Neutrogena is a good way to go, and a small sponge in the bottom of the soap dish will prevent residue buildup.

❋ There should be a clean mirror and good lighting. This is non-negotiable—applying makeup is important to women.

❋ You get extra credit for a soft, freshly laundered cotton robe.

❋ The medicine cabinet (assume that she will look inside) should contain a new toothbrush (unwrapped) for her and a relatively unsqueezed tube of toothpaste; basics (not necessarily all for her) like deodorant and shaving items, comb or hairbrush, Q-tips, cotton balls, nail clippers, tweezers, and small scissors; aspirin, Tylenol, or another pain medication; stomach settler like Pepto-Bismol; and a small medical kit containing Band-Aids, gauze pads and wrap, adhesive tape, etc.

With all this, both you and your guest should be happy. But don't forget to remove potentially embarrassing prescription bottles from the medicine cabinet before *any* visitor uses the bathroom.

THE GUESTS YOU DON'T WANT

While the bathroom seems like a quiet refuge where you can be alone with your thoughts, it's actually teeming with life. But it's not the kind of company you want to keep. Most bathrooms are warm and damp—ideal breeding grounds for dozens of microorganisms. If they go unchecked, whole civilizations of tiny creatures like bacteria, rotavirus, E. coli, salmonella, plus assorted allergens and pathogens will call it home, existing in microscopic rain forests of mold and mildew. Standing water in the toilet and on the shower floor, damp washcloths, toothbrushes, the toilet seat, sink faucets, shower curtains, and even reading materials create the perfect environment for all these microbes.

That's why the bathroom is one of two rooms in your home (your kitchen is the other) where more than a superficial cleaning is important and a good, semifrequent disinfecting is essential.

Battle of the Bathroom

Chemical weapons may have been outlawed by the Geneva Convention, but they're 100 percent cool to use in your bathroom. You can build a superb arsenal—cleaning sprays and solutions that clean and/or kill germs—with a trip to a supermarket, hardware store, or home center. Select the following products, many of which you can also use in the kitchen and elsewhere:

* Lysol Disinfectant Spray (lemon scented)
* Pine-Sol Cleaner (pine scented)
* Clorox Disinfecting Wipes
* Tilex Mildew Remover
* Soft Scrub with Bleach

DAILY CLEANING

1. Wipe off and polish the sink with a washcloth, a sponge, or toilet paper often, or as often as you see it getting a little grungy. Squirt it with a disinfecting cleaner first, if you want. This only takes a few seconds.
2. Get in the habit of spritzing the shower interior and inside of its door (or curtain) with Tilex, to prevent mildew, and Lysol or another pleasantly scented disinfectant after every use. These are five-second jobs that will keep mildew and germs at bay.
3. Keep a sponge under soap bars to minimize scum in the dish.
4. Keep the bathroom as uncluttered as you can.

WEEKLY CLEANING

Launder towels and washcloths, and give the entire bathroom a good surface cleaning:

1. Squirt bowl cleaner into the toilet, brush it around, let it stand, then flush (for more details on toilet cleaning, see page 123).
2. Spray Windex on the mirror, the windows, and the shower door, then wipe with clean cotton rags.

3. Use Soft Scrub or Formula 409 on the inside of the shower door where soap residue may build up.

4. Use Windex, Lysol, or disinfecting wipes on the countertops, the toilet tank, and the outside of the toilet bowl; wipe with a sponge, then dry with cotton rags.

5. Shake out rugs onto the floor, then sweep or vacuum the floor.

BI-WEEKLY OR MONTHLY CLEANING

1. Apply Soft Scrub to the tub interior, the wall tiles, and the grout with the Teflon side of a Scotch-Brite sponge, then rinse.

2. To disinfect, spray the tub, the tiles, and the grout with a medium-strength ammonia-water solution (about 1:8, or 2 ounces ammonia per pint water) or Lysol disinfectant sprayed right out of its own bottle.

3. To give the tub and tiles a slick, Teflon-like surface that sheds soap scum, spray them with silicon-based furniture polish or wipe with baby oil.

4. If you have hard-water residue (spots or film) on walls, glass shower doors, faucets, etc., apply Lime-A-Way with the Teflon side of a Scotch-Brite sponge, then rinse with water.

5. To keep drains free of clogs, pour in 1/2 cup baking soda and chase it with 1/2 cup white vinegar. Let it fizz for a few minutes, then pour in a kettle of boiling water.

QUARTERLY OR WHENEVER-IT-GETS-NOTICEABLY-GROSS CLEANING

1. You might have stubborn water spots on tiles or shower doors, especially if you have hard water—that is, water that's heavy on mineral and calcium particulates. First, apply Soft Scrub with a damp, Scotch-Brite sponge, and get at grout between tiles with a soft-bristled nylon brush. Let the solution stay in contact with the surface for a few minutes, then rinse and repeat if necessary. Use Lime-A-Way for very tough spots.

2. Try to avoid using abrasive cleaners like Comet on tiles and shower door glass.

3. Empty your medicine cabinet; toss away outdated medications and anything else you don't need. Remove the shelves if you can and clean the interior.

Specific Cleanups

PLASTIC SHOWER WALLS AND FLOOR

A bleach solution is the traditional weapon, but using a whitewall-tire cleaner like Bleche-White is better. It also works on grungy rubber bath mats if you have one. Get Bleche-White at your local discount store or auto-supply store. Spray or sponge onto the surface, let it work for a few minutes, then rinse off.

SHOWER CURTAIN LINER

Machine-wash with your towels, then hang it back up on the shower rod to dry. The bottom hem, the little fold along the outside edge, is often a mildew magnet. Just cut the hem off with scissors—you don't need it.

SHOWERHEAD

If the shower pressure is weaker than what you want, the showerhead may be clogging with hard-water minerals (lime or calcium), rust buildup, or tiny particulates being filtered out of the water. It should unscrew easily. Rinse it out, along with any screen filter you find.

If it's metal, apply Lime-A-Way with a sponge or a cotton cloth. Let it work, rinse again, and repeat if necessary. Metal showerheads can also be boiled in a solution of $1/2$ cup white vinegar mixed with 1 quart water to dissolve mineral deposits.

If it's plastic, soak it in a 50-50 solution of white vinegar and

---

STRATEGIC MANEUVER Stop Soap Scum

Place a small sponge into each soap dish or wall-mounted soap holder (such as in the shower). It absorbs water and soap scum runoff when it's underneath the just-used bar.

hot water for several hours. If it doesn't unscrew from the shower pipe, put the vinegar-water solution in a plastic bag and attach it over the showerhead with a rubber band or another tie.

A rubber gasket with a small hole that restricts water flow may be inserted in the showerhead fixture. If you want a stronger flow, remove the rubber gasket.

MEDICINE CABINET

Check prescription labels regularly and throw away the outdated ones. Some medicines lose potency with age, and some get stronger; neither scenario is good. Check expiration dates on over-the-counter vitamins, cold medicines, and sunscreens, and discard any that are outdated.

Empty the medicine cabinet and clean the interior at least quarterly with a damp washcloth.

TOILET

Cleaning the toilet is demeaning and disgusting but, alas, inevitable. Consider the alternative: In some countries they don't even have toilets. So just roll up your sleeves, turn around your ball cap, and get it done. Semiweekly is best, but weekly is realistic.

CLEANING THE BOWL

1. If necessary, flush it.
2. One option: Dump in a dash of Sani-Flush or a similar toilet bowl cleaner, let it work for a few moments, then brush, including under the rim, and flush to rinse.
3. A kinder, gentler option: First lower the water level by pushing your brush toward and into the drain, or shut off the water supply to the tank (the valve near the wall) and flush. Add a disinfectant cleaner (a mildly abrasive gel like Clorox Toilet Bowl cleaner, or something like Comet for tough stains) and work around with your brush. Let it work for a few minutes or more, and flush to rinse.
4. If you have persistent stains, try a cleaning tablet in the tank. These last for several weeks and chlorinate the water so it's

always cleaning. You'll still have to clean with a brush occasionally, however. Or pour a cup of chlorine bleach in and let it work. Don't let the dog drink out of the bowl anymore, though.

CLEANING THE REST OF THE TOILET

1. Spray the entire outer surface (including the seat and the lid and their hinges, the top edge of the bowl, and the base) with a disinfectant cleaner.
2. Let it work for a few minutes, then wipe down with a sponge and dry with a cotton rag.

Plumbing

Many "simple" plumbing jobs I thought would take half an hour have burned up entire Saturdays with numerous trips to the hardware store. Sadly, you never know you should have called a pro until it's too late. Since bathrooms have more plumbing than any other room in the house, here's some manly advice to help you sidestep at least *some* potential problems.

BATHROOM SINK

PREVENTIVE MEASURES

* Run plenty of water when washing soap, shaving cream, lotion, and any other potentially clogging stuff down the drain.
* To keep the drain free-running, use the baking soda–vinegar–boiling water trick (page 104). If it's not free-running after this, try using a plunger to clear a clogged drain; or remove the P-trap in the drain and clear out debris; or call a plumber.

TUB OR SHOWER

PREVENTIVE MEASURES

Try all the tricks described for the bathroom sink, except for fooling with the P-trap, which is probably inaccessible anyway.

TOILET

If it's clogged:

* First use a plunger to try to clear the debris.
* If a plunger fails, try a plumber's snake.
* Still no dice? Go pro.

MANDATORY ADVICE
Sometimes It's Smart to Go Pro

Never be too macho or hardheaded to call a professional plumber. Plumbing is not easy, and trying to solve tricky problems just isn't worth the time or frustration it's likely to involve. I've personally wasted an incredible amount of time trying to be a do-it-myselfer, attempting to fix drips that turned into nightmares.

SHEET
HAPPENS

Blowing Through the Bedroom

If you haven't been in the military or in prison, you probably don't know how to make a bed properly. While the finished product doesn't have to be a work of art, I think that making your bed daily can be a very important cornerstone of a personal-neatness program. When you get into the habit of doing it first thing every morning, the entire bedroom looks neater. A well-made bed also creates the impression that your life is in order, and it has a positive impact on your frame of mind. An unmade bed has just the opposite effect. There's probably some kind of rule like Murphy's Law about this. The point is: The minute or two it takes to make your bed in the morning is a great investment in the rest of your day.

Cleaning the bedroom is pretty much a no-brainer, even for a guy. You just have to vacuum occasionally, dust when you start to see it, use Windex for the mirrors—all tasks that were discussed in Chapter 4. What's more, your bedroom is most likely a relatively small space and should be fairly easy to keep neat and clean. So there are really only three room-specific housekeeping issues to address here: bed, clothes closet, and clothing storage inside dresser drawers.

The Bed

Your bed should feel good when you're in it, and look good when you're not. First, buy a high-quality mattress and box spring— together they're called a sleep set—if you don't already own them. Get at least a double, possibly a queen or a king. And firm. Remember, your comfort is the key. You spend eight hours a day there, after all, so don't cut corners on quality to save a few dollars. You'll just be cheating yourself out of a good night's rest.

MATTRESS CARE AND CLEANING

To extend the life of your mattress, it should be *turned* periodically, ideally every two to three months. But knowing men, twice a year will do just fine. Turning your mattress is similar to rotating your car's tires: it equalizes wear—in this case, the weight of your body compressing the mattress coils and padding. Over time,

STRATEGIC **MAN**EUVER
What Women Really Want

There was once a time (probably in the 1970s) when a man would try to impress a lady by showing her a snapshot of his Corvette. But the next time you have an opportunity to chat with an attractive female, casually mention that you have on your bed 400 thread–count sheets of 100 percent Egyptian combed cotton. (First, though, buy these things.) It may take a bit of ingenuity to steer the conversation around to your bed linens, but you can do it. Having such luxurious bedding demonstrates that you're a man of discriminating tastes. It also gets the topic of "bed" out there.

HOME **MAN**AGEMENT TIP
Use Your Head—Store Under Your Bed

The space under your bed represents great storage space, so why not use it to the max? Get two or three large, flat plastic containers to use as drawers you can slide in and out from beneath the bed. The containers just have to clear the lowest edge of the frame in order to work, so measure the frame's clearance off the floor before you shop for containers. Even cardboard boxes cut to the right height will do just fine, except that they don't slide quite as well as plastic. Fill them with sweaters, T-shirts, shorts, jeans, extra bedding . . . just about anything. It's a great place to stow clothing that's being stored between seasons, too.

a mattress can develop a permanent indentation unless you turn it occasionally.

If the mattress has a pillow-top, just rotate the head and foot positions. If it's the same on both sides, flip it *over* as well as *around*. This will mean you're rotating it four ways: turning it around from head to foot and then flipping it over from top side to bottom side. To keep track of your rotations on the four-position mattress, put masking tape at all four ends, facing up, and write in numbers 1 through 4. Then simply turn to the next number and put it at the head of the bed, facing up, every time you rotate the mattress.

Purchase a fitted mattress pad to place over the mattress—it has elastic edges to ensure a snug fit on mattress corners. For additional softness on a firm mattress, you can use a portable foam-rubber "eggshell" pad between the mattress and your fitted pad. These have a series of mogul-like ridges that provide a few more degrees of comfort. You can find them at just about any store that has a domestics department.

To clean and freshen the mattress, try this trick each time you take off the bedding and sheets for laundering or every time you rotate the mattress: Sprinkle some baking soda or carpet-freshener powder over the mattress surface; leave it for as long as you like, a few minutes or a few hours; then vacuum it off with the machine's extension hose and the upholstery nozzle attachment.

FUTONS

A futon is a mattress that has no coils, just a thick padding of cotton batting or foam rubber. It usually rests on a simple wooden frame. Rotating your futon mattress every once in a while is probably a good idea, similar to fluffing a down pillow. To clean and deodorize a futon, use the same method described above for a regular mattress: baking soda or carpet cleaner, and a good airing-out as often as possible.

MANDATORY ADVICE
Keep Your Bedroom Clean and Simple

A man's bedroom should be a relaxing, restful place that promotes a good night's sleep and has a little style to boot. A comfortable, inviting sanctuary that an attractive female guest would not be afraid to enter and, perhaps, to stay awhile. Now *that's* the stuff dreams are made of.

For this to happen, you should maintain a minimum threshold of cleanliness, order, and good taste: no unmade bed, no linens that haven't seen a washing machine since your last birthday, and no black-light posters, red silk bedspreads, or mirrored ceilings. Please. This isn't a decorating book, but you can hardly go wrong with earthy colors, warm lighting, a big white comforter, and a few accent pillows on a neatly made bed.

STRATEGIC **MAN**EUVER Sheet Shortcut

Here's a clever way to instantly align the flat top sheet when you're making the bed. You won't have to goof around getting both sides to hang evenly or figuring out the perfect amount of hem to leave up near the pillows:

❋ First, get the sheet aligned the old trial-and-error way.

❋ Then take a permanent marker and make two small dots on the sheet in each corner near the foot of the bed. A stitch of colored thread or a couple of small safety pins work, too.

❋ You'll now be able to take this sheet out of the dryer, whip it onto the bed, and get it perfectly aligned using those dots, threads, or pins for guidance.

BED LINENS

Your sheets and pillowcases should be made of cotton or linen. Cotton is the best all-season choice, cool in the summer and pleasant to the touch—soft and natural. You might choose cotton flannel sheets in the winter. Some housekeeping books say you have to iron cotton sheets because they're prone to wrinkling. But avoiding this is easy: just take them out of the dryer *right away* after they're done and put them onto the bed.

Do not buy polyester sheets. This is the fabric that's cool in winter, warm in summer—just the opposite of what you want. Cotton with a small blend of polyester should be okay, striking a reasonable balance between comfort and easy care (read: fewer wrinkles).

Sheets and pillowcases should be laundered every week, ideally. Realistically, for guys, every ten days to two weeks (or, pushing the boundaries of decency and hygiene, every three weeks). Just don't wait until you can actually *see* that your bedding needs washing, that's all.

STRATEGIC **MAN**EUVER
Making the Bed Faster

Hotel maids have this down: For maximum efficiency when changing the sheets, they work one side of the bed until it's almost done—sheets on, bedspread on, pillows in position—then move to the other side and do the same thing, then back to finish the first side. That's one round trip from one side of the bed to the other, instead of the countless ones a man can make when putting the bed back together.

MAKING THE BED

Can't bounce a quarter off the top of your tightly made bed? No problem: This isn't the army. Just doing an efficient, functional job that looks good is plenty fine. Here's how:

1. Put on the bottom *fitted* sheet (this is the one with elastic corners made to fit over the mattress corners), one corner at a time. If it has shrunk a bit, pull it onto diagonally opposite corners: lower left and upper right, followed by lower right and upper left.
2. Unfurl the top *flat* sheet across the bed. If it has a pattern, put the patterned side down. The larger hem should be at the head of the bed. Get it aligned with equal "hang" on either side of the bed and enough hem at the head of the bed to fold down over your blanket.
3. Tuck the flat sheet in at the foot of the bed and securely tuck in the sides.
4. Add the (optional) blanket, tucking it in under the foot of the bed the same way as you did the sheet, and fold down the top hem of the sheet over the blanket.
5. Toss a big comforter over the whole thing and straighten it.
6. Dress up the bed with a few accent pillows toward the head of

the bed. This is certainly optional, but it helps the bed look good when not in use. Even though you may not really care, women do.

7. Enjoy!

You can build on this foundation to develop your own manly method for speedy bed making. Of course, it's always easier and quicker when you have a bunkmate to help, but the ball is in your court on that one.

PILLOWS

In descending order of price, you can purchase pillows filled with down, a down-feather combination, feathers, polyester fiberfill, or foam. Here's the heads-up on pillows:

* Choose the type of pillow that's most comfortable for you, unless allergies are an issue.
* Some books advise laundering pillows every two or three months. I say you can do it twice a year, and like it.
* Follow the instructions on the pillow's care tag for washing and drying. Some experts suggest that down pillows should be dry-cleaned.

STRATEGIC **MAN**EUVER
A Quick Way to Keep Pillows Fresh

For a fast freshening-up of your pillows instead of a full-blown washing:

* Put one or two pillows in the dryer with a fabric softener sheet.
* Set the temp on low or "delicate," and tumble them for twenty minutes or so.
* This should help you procrastinate for a little longer before laundering your pillows as described here. It also works for blankets, bedspreads, and comforters.

* You have to wash pillows two at a time so your washing machine's inner tub will stay in balance when it's in the spin cycle. A soaked pillow is very heavy and can throw the spinning tub out of balance if there's only one pillow in the washer, or if two of them get jammed on one side of the tub.

* To dry pillows, toss them into the dryer and set it on medium to low heat. Take the time to do a thorough job; make sure you completely dry out the moisture that encourages mildew and a musty odor.

* When drying pillows, take them out of the dryer every twenty minutes or so to fluff them. A few tennis balls in the dryer help to fluff pillows, too.

* You can also hang pillows on a line or rack to dry them. But that sounds like it would take a long time, and therefore it's very unmanly.

BEDSPREAD

The smartest bedspread choice for the manly bedroom is a big comforter you can just toss over the pulled-up sheets. Straighten it up, smooth it out, and you're done with "making" the bed. There's no tucking, no folding, and precious little aligning involved. This is a major-league timesaver. It looks great, too: tailored, masculine, and inviting. Select a plain white, neutral, or light-colored comforter. Place a few decorative pillows in front of the ones you sleep on, and it's an instant fashion statement.

A removable cover that's easy to slip off and launder is highly recommended. If your comforter doesn't have one, your investment in an outer cover will be richly returned in what you'll save on dry-cleaning. You should put the cover through the wash monthly, especially if you like to snack in bed.

The Clothes Closet

FIRST, UNCLUTTER

Here's how to deal with your hang-ups, and all the other stuff in your closet. Take everything out and put into a big garbage bag anything you haven't worn in at least a year, items that are hopelessly out of style, or clothes and shoes you simply don't want anymore. Then put the remaining contents back in. Improvement is guaranteed.

The only word of warning is to make certain that when you start this project, you're prepared to keep working on it until it's finished. Cleaning out your closet a little at a time doesn't work. If you stop before you're done, you tend never to get back to it.

SMART CLOSET STORAGE

Make the most of your closet space by following a few easy guidelines:

✳ Hang like items together in their own sections: sport coats, slacks, dress shirts, casual shirts.

✳ Hang items with all the hanger hooks pointing away from you, toward the back wall of the closet. This way you can take multiple items off the rack at the same time.

✳ Try to use plastic or wooden hangers rather than the metal ones you get back with your dry cleaning. Metal hangers can rust and discolor clothing, or create funny-looking creases on the shoulders of shirts.

✳ Fasten the top button on hanging shirts. Otherwise the fabric between the top button and the first button down will sag and lose its shape.

✳ Don't hang sweaters or other knits by the shoulders if you can help it. If you must hang them, drape them over the padded bar of the hanger to avoid stretching and misshaping the shoulders.

✳ Don't pack hanging items tightly together. Leave things loose and airy and your clothes will have fewer wrinkles.

✳ Fold sweaters and jeans, then stack them neatly on a shelf above the hanging clothes. If you don't have a shelf, add one. That's valuable space, not to be wasted.

✳ If you have room, put in *two* upper shelves, with the higher one about 12 inches above the lower one. You don't want to stack clothing too high, or it's tough to get garments at the bottom of the stack without demolishing the rest of the pile.

✳ Don't store clothes in plastic bags or other airtight containers, even the ones you get back from the dry cleaner (unless you're going to pack them right away for travel). A little air circulation is good for garments and helps prevent mildew.

* Get a shoe rack, either a door-mounted one (where each shoe has its own hook or pocket) or a horizontal floor platform that's placed underneath hanging items. As a guy, you probably have only about three pairs of shoes anyway, but using a rack beats throwing them on the floor willy-nilly.

* You can find space-saving storage racks for ties and belts, which usually hang from the horizontal closet bar. They're highly recommended because they keep these items together in one place.

CLOSET CLEANING AND MAINTENANCE

Clean your clothes closets thoroughly about twice a year (spring and fall) to prevent mildew and keep clothes fresh. Don't put damp items in the closet; added humidity promotes mildew and eventually produces a musty odor. If you can already detect a musty smell inside your closet, here's what to do:

1. Remove everything.
2. Air out the closet. Leave a lightbulb on to dry it, and use a fan to circulate air.
3. Launder or dry-clean all clothing that requires it.
4. Before putting clothes back, place an open container of baking soda on a shelf or hang an old nylon stocking or sock filled with cat litter. Both help to absorb odors and moisture.

MANDATORY ADVICE
When, Why, and How to Line Dresser Drawers

In less expensive dressers, the wood may contain chemicals that can stain clothes—especially if there's any moisture present. The solution: Either buy a better class of dresser or line the drawer interiors with sheets of plastic or moisture-resistant shelf paper.

The Dresser

Dresser drawers are meant to store clothing that doesn't have to hang or can't be conveniently stacked on an open shelf: underwear, socks, T-shirts, shorts, swimsuits, and the like. Of course, things that you can stack or hang (sweaters, slacks, shirts, belts) may also go in there. Some tips:

* Don't jam items tightly into drawers. Instead, fold and arrange clothing loosely but neatly. The idea is to allow airflow, just like in a closet, to minimize mustiness and mildew.
* *Roll up* items like shirts and pants to avoid wrinkles and extra, unwanted creases. This is also a good tip for packing luggage.
* To keep drawers smelling fresh, place an unwrapped bar of soap inside with the clothes, or add a fabric-softener sheet.
* Before storing items for the season, launder or dry-clean everything.
* When you take clothes out of seasonal storage, toss them into the dryer and run it with no heat for ten minutes or so to freshen the items and remove wrinkles.

GOING LOW
Carpet and Flooring

The most famous of all treatments for carpet stains is to apply a little club soda. But guys don't have any—we drank it all with our scotch.

Thanks to gravity, almost all dirt and dust in your home eventually winds up on your floors and carpets. If that's not enough, we constantly walk all over them, track mud and grime onto them, drag our feet across them, let our pets claw them up, and spill sticky foods and colorful beverages on them.

Floors have it tough, yet underneath all that filth they can be beautiful. And caring for your vinyl, tile, and wood floors, and your carpeting will not only bring out their most attractive attributes, it will prolong their lives and save you big bucks in the long run. (For emergencies, check out "Treating the Most Common Man-Stains on Carpeting" on pages 152–154.)

Vinyl, Linoleum, Rubber, and Asphalt

Vinyl can be described with three words every guy loves to hear: virtually maintenance-free. It's the toughest, most versatile, and easiest-to-clean type of floor. And most of the vinyl flooring produced and installed within the last thirty years falls into the "no-wax" category. Is this getting better all the time or what?

You find vinyl flooring in a lot of kitchens because it's consid-

STRATEGIC **MAN**EUVER
Use Prevention As Your Cure

We live in a big, dirty world. It's no surprise that almost all the soil that gets into your house and onto your carpets and floors is tracked in from outside. So it makes sense to stop grime at the door, and there are several good ways to do it.

Use the "scraper" doormats.
Look up a few "Janitorial Equipment & Supplies" stores in the Yellow Pages and get some commercial "scraper" mats—the ones with the wiry coiled-vinyl facing. Put one outside your most heavily trafficked entryways and one inside (if the inside mat will be placed on carpeting, it should have a rubber backing so moisture doesn't seep through). These mats work great at scraping most dirt, dust, and mud off of shoes before it can be tracked inside.

Ask guests to remove their shoes before entering.
Some of the more "radical chic" cleaning books suggest that you make family and guests remove their footwear at the door, Japanese-style. This simple custom goes a long way toward saving rugs, carpeting, and especially hardwood floors. While it's an excellent way to eliminate tracked-in dirt, it may be too "Felix" for most guys. And your visitors might expect sushi to be served.

Keep your garage floor clean.
If you have an attached garage, sweep it out regularly—especially the area right in front of the door leading into the house. It doesn't take long for your garage floor to get dirty and gritty, particularly in the wintertime when your car is often dripping with melting snow.

ered a little softer than wood and tile; it's more comfortable to stand on. It would be completely out of place in the bedroom, living room, and especially an entryway, where its pliability would be no match for the high traffic and tracked-in grit.

When talking about vinyl, several other types of flooring—linoleum, rubber, and asphalt—can be lumped into the conversation because they can all be cared for in the same general way, using the same products. These floors are all softer than wood and tile, so some protective measures will help to avoid any scratching and undue wear.

TOP TIPS

* Sweep frequently to keep abrasive soil and grit off the surface of the floor, and damp-mop about once a week.
* Place floor mats at entrances, both inside and out, to cut down on the dirt that's tracked in from outside. (This is a good tip no matter what kind of floors you have.)
* Put rugs in spots where you know there'll be lots of wear or traffic, like in front of your kitchen sink and at entrances to the room.
* Use plastic caps or glides on the feet of chairs and tables.
* Wear your golf spikes as little as possible indoors.

BASIC CARE AND CLEANING

* Damp-mop regularly using a gallon of water with a little all-purpose cleaner added. Nothing fancy: $1/2$ cup Pine-Sol or even a few drops of dishwashing liquid is fine.
* Always sweep the dry floor *before* you damp-mop to get most of the grittiest soil up. You could also go over the floor with your vacuum and a dust-brush attachment.
* After mopping, let the floor air-dry, or wipe it dry with a soft cotton cloth.
* For serious spots or smears, scrub *lightly* with the nylon face of a Scotch-Brite sponge before you damp-mop.
* Remember, damp-mop only. If you use a wet mop, the puddles of solution you leave might seep into the floor seams and loosen the edges of the flooring.

POLISHING

"No-wax" floors will keep their great looks for years with minimal care, but over time—or if you have a lot of traffic, tracked-in dirt, and activity—your vinyl floor can lose its glossy finish. If some spots start showing a little wear, you can add a layer of wax or floor polish for extra protection and for cosmetic purposes.

* Get a brand-name polish at the hardware store, or purchase a heavy-duty polish at a janitorial supply store. Ask for recommendations if you're unsure of product quality.
* Always read labels or ask questions before you buy to make sure you're getting the right stuff for your particular floor.
* After the first layer is applied, you can just touch up the main traffic areas as needed.
* After you've polished a floor, try to avoid cleaners that contain ammonia. They will take the polish off or dull the finish.

MINOR REPAIRS

The seams in vinyl floors are the points most prone to loosening and lifting. When this happens, take care of it as soon as you can because it's only going to get worse.

1. Slide a thin putty knife under the loose seam and lift it.
2. Remove old, loose adhesive.
3. Apply fresh adhesive (the material for floors is called mastic) under the edge with the putty knife and press the flooring down. Wipe off any excess adhesive that squeezes out with a damp sponge.
4. Put wax paper over the repair, weigh it down with a book or another heavy, flat object, and let it cure for at least twenty-four hours.

Ceramic Tile

Tile is tough, attractive, and easy to maintain and clean. Just vacuum or sweep, damp-mop using water with a dash of dishwashing detergent in it, rinse, and let dry. With such low-maintenance requirements, you might think you'd want it in every room, but tile is most appropriate for entryways and bathrooms: it's decora-

HOME **MAN**AGEMENT TIP
"Get Down" for Best Results

My entryway and bathroom floors (both tile) aren't huge, so rather than damp-mopping them I get down on my hands and knees to wash them. This seems to get them a lot cleaner than the mop does, and it's almost as quick.

If you want to go this route, sweep or vacuum thoroughly first. Then use a damp sponge or a cotton cloth to wash a swath of floor, then dry it with another cotton terry cloth. You can also touch up the baseboards while you're down there. Prevent gnarly, knobby "altar-boy's knees" by kneeling on a foam pad made especially for gardeners who spend a lot of time on their knees; they're available at gardening and home stores.

tive while being tough, waterproof, and easy to clean. Tile wouldn't be your first choice for the living room or bedroom, where the tactile softness of carpet or the visual warmth of wood is more appropriate.

Ceramic tile is the catchall name for tiling made from the earthy ingredients of clay or silica, then formed and hardened by "firing" it at high temperatures. Most tile you see these days has a glaze—a glossy coating that's very hard and durable, almost impervious to stains and moisture. Over many years it may wear down and get a little dull, or become somewhat nicked up. But hey, so do you.

Tile without glaze, like quarry tile, is more porous and might require sealing or more frequent cleaning, even though it's still a very low-maintenance choice for flooring.

You see tiles on the walls of kitchens and bathrooms for decorative effect. Since glazed tile is very stain-resistant, it has become popular for kitchen countertops. Porcelain used for sinks and toilets is a glazed tile as well. But here we'll just zero in on floor tiles.

BASIC CARE AND CLEANING

❋ Sweep or vacuum often.

❋ Be especially vigilant about keeping sand off the floor. Its gritty little particles are about the only common substance that's just as hard as the glaze, and it will have the biggest impact on wear.

❋ Damp-mop about once a week using water and a little all-purpose cleaner or a cleaner that's specially formulated for tile. Then rinse with clean water.

❋ You can let the floor air-dry, but if the tiles appear dull afterward it might be residue from the cleaning solution you used. Polish up the floor with a cotton terry cloth or towel—you can just move it around on the floor with your foot.

❋ Never use scouring powders or abrasive tools like steel brushes on your tiles. Either one can scratch and ruin the glaze finish. If you must scrub, use a nylon-bristle brush.

GROUT

Grout, the adhesive applied between tile seams, is also extremely hard but very rough, porous, and more prone to stains. Here are some tips to keep cleaning easy:

❋ Apply a liquid sealant to make grout less porous and more resistant to discoloration.

❋ Grout comes in many different shades to complement the tile. Light-colored grouts are common. Very dark grouts look good, too, and choosing a dark tone in the first place minimizes the visual effects of any staining that may occur.

❋ Quick cleanup of any foods or beverages spilled onto grout will keep serious staining to a minimum.

❋ If you do happen to get an ugly stain, mold, or mildew on white or light-colored grout, try this: Mix a solution of $3/4$ cup bleach (don't splash it onto clothing!) to 1 gallon water. Put a little of the solution on an inconspicuous area to make sure it doesn't ruin the tile. Let it work on the stain for a minute or two, then scrub lightly with a nylon brush or an old toothbrush, and rinse with clear water. You can also try a similar semiabrasive cleaner such as Soft Scrub with Bleach, but always test it on an out-of-the-way area before going whole-hog with it.

Hardwood Floors

Today's hardwood floors are better and more beautiful than ever. The prefinished ones are impregnated with acrylics and polymers that make them both tough and good-looking. Unfinished ones can be treated with polyurethane to be just as shiny and resilient, as well as protected with wax or polish.

If you're not certain what kind of finish is on your wood floor, find out before you try to clean it and proceed accordingly. If you wax a urethane floor or use a water-based cleaner on a wax finish, you might be in for some major stripping, sanding, and refinishing if you ever want your floor to shine again. But regardless of the finish, there are several rules that hold true for all wood floors when it comes to providing loving care for them.

BASIC CARE AND CLEANING

ALL WOOD FLOORS

* Dust often and sweep or vacuum frequently to keep them free of dust, dirt, and grit—all of which are major causes of deterioration of a wood floor's finish. Use scraper doormats at entrances to your home to keep dirt out in the first place.
* Use water sparingly to clean wood floors. Although it's okay to go over your floor with a very light, very occasional damp-mopping, I prefer to dry and buff the floor by hand as I finish mopping, using my trusty old cotton terry cloths or towels.
* Never let wood floors stay wet with water or anything else. Mop up all spills ASAP.
* Do not slide furniture across a wood floor; it causes scratches. Don't set furniture feet directly on wood, either. Instead use coasters, sliders, press-on felt, or even rugs at the points where the furniture rests on the floor.
* If you're not sure what finish has been applied to each wooden floor in your home, find a hardwood floor specialist in the Yellow Pages and ask him to take a look at your floor, make some recommendations, and give you the "free estimate."

WOOD FLOORS WITH A URETHANE FINISH

Urethane, polyurethane, and water-based finishes all fall into this category, and they're the most low-maintenance wood floors of all. They're also the most popular finish.

* Urethane-finished floors should not be waxed, but they can be damp-mopped occasionally.
* Sweep or vacuum (with the dust attachment) as much as possible.
* You can spot-clean scuffs and other marks before washing the entire floor with a product intended just for this, or rub the scuffs lightly with a dab of mineral spirits—a cleaning solvent—on a terry cloth.
* When you use a product specifically made to clean urethane-finished floors, read the label guidelines first.
* Otherwise, use a very mild soap-and-water solution to damp-mop, going with the grain of the wood. Rinse the mop in clean water whenever needed (a double-compartment bucket is perfect for this).
* Then dry by hand with a terry cloth or rag if at all possible—it's worth the trouble.

MANDATORY ADVICE
Things Not to Do to Urethane Floors

* Do not wax these floors.
* Never use abrasive cleaners, ammonia, or any other chemical cleaners. All of them can ruin the finish.
* Don't apply Pledge, Endust, or any other spray duster/polisher intended for use on furniture; these products will create very slippery conditions. And soaps that contain oil can leave a dulling, sticky residue. (Except for Murphy Oil Soap, which doesn't really contain oil; it's just made from oil. Go figure.)

WOOD FLOORS WITH A WAX FINISH

These "soft" floors are pretty much out of vogue because they require more care than urethane-finished floors. Wax is applied and absorbed into the wood, protecting it from scratches, stains, and dirt, and it has a satin look rather than a shiny one. You'll still be able to feel the wood grain with your hand if you have a waxed floor as opposed to one with a polyurethane finish. If you have a waxed floor:

* Natural wood floors should be waxed or polished regularly; these floors should not be damp-mopped.

* When the finish looks dull or you can see spots with a marred, rubbed-off look, try buffing the floor with a cotton terry rag. If it's still in need of improvement, apply a one-step clean-and-polish product with a wax applicator. Rub it on in the direction of the grain, let it dry for a half hour or so, then buff with a soft cotton cloth.

* Wax the floor about once a year to protect it against moisture. First remove the wax with a store-bought wax-removing product or with mineral spirits, then reapply one or two coats of liquid or paste wax. Read the labels: Make sure the wax is specifically intended for wood floors. You'll damage the finish if you use furniture polish or solvents meant for urethane-finished wood floors, or a wax that's made for resilient (no-wax) or tile floors.

* Rub heel marks and other scuffs with a small amount of paste floor wax and very fine steel wool, then buff.

* Again, don't use water to clean this type of floor, and keep it as dry as possible. Don't damp-mop or use ammonia or vinegar between waxings.

Carpeting

After decades of research, development, and a healthy application of space-age technology, carpeting fibers have become more durable and easier to care for and keep clean. The latest generation of fibers is extremely resilient. In fact, a carpet-cleaning professional once told me that white and other light-hued carpeting is more resistant to dirt and stains than any other colors, because manufacturers have paid the most attention to these popular shades.

Another surprise: The dirt and debris that's least visible on your carpets can cause more long-term damage than the stuff you can actually see, and it can dramatically shorten the life of your floor coverings. The tiny particles of soil that start out on top of your carpet eventually work their way deeper and deeper into the fibers. There they act like sharp-edged little cutting machines that slice, grind, and break down the carpet fibers every time you walk across the floor. The result is a less-resilient carpet that loses its finish, stain resistance, and good looks more quickly than it has to.

REGULAR VACUUMING

This is the key to keeping your carpets in top shape, and a good deep-cleaning once or twice a year also helps immensely. Vacuuming tools and techniques are covered in Chapters 2 and 4; here are the specifics for carpets:

* Use a model with a twirling beater-bar brush that loosens dirt and vibrates it to the carpet surface, where it's swept into the vacuum. Vacuums that use only suction, like a shop vac, will not get out the deep-down soil and grit.

STRATEGIC **MAN**EUVER
Squeaking Out a Solution

Getting new wall-to-wall carpet over that ratty old wood floor? Get rid of the squeaks first. After the carpet's down, it's too late.

* Walk the entire floor, marking squeaky spots with tape.
* Sprinkle talcum powder or powdered graphite into the floorboard cracks around each area that squeaks.
* Brush the powder into the cracks, and wipe away what's left.

* Vacuum slowly. Easy, sweeping motions are much more effective than quick swipes. Go over each swath of carpeting two or three times, using overlapping strokes. Some experts suggest that making up to seven passes over each area delivers the best results. I am not one of them; fewer passes are probably fine.

* Spend more time vacuuming high-traffic areas. That's where the most soil will be deposited. Pay special attention to entryways. Keep them swept clean on the outside and well vacuumed on the inside. Use scraper mats or throw rugs in these areas.

CLEANING AND SHAMPOOING

You can rent carpet-shampoo machines at a vacuum store or a rental center, but the equipment is sometimes old and rickety. These overused units often don't deliver sufficient rinsing power and suction to get all the soap and water out of carpeting; and on carpeting, dried soap residue is a *dirt magnet*.

If you rent a machine, it should be in top shape and from a reliable source who backs the results. Or, call a reputable professional and use a company that can at least afford an ad in the Yellow Pages.

Between deep cleanings you can use a dry powder to clean carpeting. Capture is a well-known brand available at janitorial-supply stores, and you can get Carpet Fresh and similar products at the supermarket. Baking soda will do in a pinch. Just sprinkle these on, brush in, and vacuum.

STAINS AND SPILLS

There are some tried-and-true treatment tips for stains and spills on carpeting. This advice applies to all situations:

1. Act fast! Don't let the spill or stain dry and set into the fabric.
2. Initially, blot up as much of the offending substance as possible using a cotton rag or a paper towel, working from the outside of the stain inward.
3. Always blot, don't scrub. No matter how tough your carpet is, scrubbing tends to wreck its nap and texture. Patience and repetition is a lot more effective than brute strength.

STRATEGIC **MAN**EUVER
Using and Cleaning Area Rugs

Small area rugs placed in strategic spots—heavily trafficked routes across the carpet or in front of entryway doors—will save lots of cleaning, not to mention wear and tear on carpeting. To clean area rugs:

* You can toss some area rugs into the laundry, but you have to vacuum others. Pay attention to the manufacturer's instructions on cleaning and maintenance.
* To vacuum a small area rug, stand on one end of it and push the vacuum over the other end. Then, on the back stroke, lift the beater bar on a canister vacuum or tilt your upright vacuum back on its wheels.
* If the rug has fringe, use your hose attachment with the upholstery tool to avoid getting strands tangled in the vacuum's rotating brush.
* Vacuum both sides of an area rug unless it's rubber-backed. The rubber-backed ones usually need laundering.
* Laundering area rugs: Use cold water, then shake the rug out before putting it into a dryer set on "cool" or "air dry."

4. Start simple. First apply plain water and blot that up before moving up to vinegar-water or detergent-water solutions or chemical spot removers.
5. Before applying a store-bought stain-removal product, read the instructions carefully, test it on an inconspicuous area of the carpet, and don't hesitate to call the 800 number on the product's label for suggestions.
6. Be patient. Once applied, give the stuff a few minutes to work.
7. You'll want to scrub, but don't. Just blot.
8. Rinse the area with plain water when you're done, and blot it up once more.

The Inevitable Carpet Spot and Stain Removal Guide

Every cleaning book features one of these guides,* but *Clean Like a Man* will take a timesaving, nontraditional approach to the exercise of removing stains.

There are three kinds of carpet stains—water-based, special water-based, and oil-based. They're caused by specific liquids or solids; each requires a different treatment approach.

The lists of stains in this chapter will help you "spot" the remedy fast. Simply find your stain, then treat it by following the directions that appear right below it. Also consult "Treating the Most Common Man-Stains on Carpeting" on pages 152–154.

Here are some items and solutions you'll need to remove most carpet spots:

✽ Towels: white paper towels or white terry towels
✽ Spray bottles for applying solutions evenly
✽ Isopropyl rubbing alcohol
✽ A spoon and a dull knife
✽ A weight like a brick or a wastebasket filled with books

Solutions used in the following carpet-stain treatments:

✽ Detergent solution: 1/4 teaspoon clear hand-dishwashing detergent that does not contain lanolin mixed with 1 cup water (safe detergents include Dawn and Joy)
✽ Ammonia solution: 1 tablespoon clear household ammonia mixed with 1/2 cup water
✽ Vinegar solution: 1/3 cup white vinegar mixed with 2/3 cup water
✽ OxiClean solution: 1/2 to 1 tablespoon OxiClean mixed with 1 pint water.

---

*Most of the information in the Inevitable Carpet Spot- and Stain-Removal Guide comes from the 3M Scotchgard website: cms.3m.com/cms/US, as well as the site sponsored by Wear-Dated Carpet Fiber from Solutia (formerly Monsanto). Always read and follow the care instructions and any warnings provided by the carpet manufacturer. Rugs and carpets with natural fibers and/or certain dyes may require special treatment. If in doubt, contact a cleaning professional for advice and/or service.

MANDATORY ADVICE
Treating the Most Common Man-Stains on Carpeting

BEER

Blot up as much as you can right away with a white paper towel or a cotton rag, then sponge the spot with plain water or a vinegar solution. Blot from the outside in. Apply a detergent solution, rinse with plain water, cover with a pad of paper towels or cotton rags weighted down by a brick, and allow to dry. If any stain remains, spray on the OxiClean solution on page 151, leave for ten minutes, blot, and repeat until the stain is gone.

BARBECUE SAUCE, STEAK SAUCE, KETCHUP

Scrape up any residue with a spoon, then blot with a cotton towel. Apply plain water, blot from the outside in, and repeat several times. Apply the vinegar solution on page 151, blot, and repeat. If any stain remains, apply the OxiClean solution on page 151, leave for ten minutes, blot, and repeat. If any stain remains, apply Resolve or Capture according to the label directions.

COFFEE

Blot with a cotton towel to remove as much of the stain as possible, then neutralize with a vinegar solution sprayed onto the spot. Blot. Apply the detergent solution on page 151, and work it in by blotting. If the spot is coming out, continue until it's removed. Rinse with tap water and blot. Spray with plain water, cover with a pad of paper towels or cotton rags weighted down by a brick, and allow to dry.

COLA

Blot with a towel, then neutralize with the ammonia solution on page 151. Apply the solution using a spray bottle, but do not wet the backing. Blot to remove excess moisture. Apply a small quantity of the detergent solution on page 151 and work it in. Continue to apply the detergent solution and blot until the spot is removed. Spray with tap water, cover with a pad of paper towels weighted down by a brick, and allow to dry.

PIZZA, NACHO CHEESE SAUCE, FRIED FOODS, CHIPS, OILY DRESSINGS, AND MEAT JUICE

Blot up or scrape off as much of the residue as possible. Apply isopropyl rubbing alcohol to a clean white cotton cloth, a white paper towel, or a cotton ball. Blot. Don't let the alcohol penetrate into the carpet backing. If the stain is still visible after a few tries, apply the detergent solution on page 151 to the spot. Blot. Repeat if it's working. Spray with tap water and blot to remove moisture. Cover with a pad of paper towels, put a weight on top, and allow to dry. If any stain remains, apply OxiClean, Resolve, or Capture according to the label directions.

GRAVY

Blot or scrape up any residue. Apply isopropyl rubbing alcohol to a clean white cotton cloth, a white paper towel, or a cotton ball. Blot until the spot is removed or no color is transferred to the cloth. If the spot isn't coming out, apply a small quantity of the detergent solution on page 151 to the spot. Blot to work the solution in. If the spot is coming out, repeat until the spot is removed. Spray lightly with water, apply a weighted pad, and allow to dry. If any stain remains, apply OxiClean, Resolve, or Capture according to the label directions.

MUSTARD

It's a very tough stain to start with, and almost impossible to remove once it dries. So act fast. Scrape away any residue, add a few drops of vinegar, wait, then rinse with cold water and blot. You may want to call a professional sooner rather than later. You may have to replace the stained area with a patch.

SALSA, TOMATO SAUCE

Remove any residue. Apply isopropyl rubbing alcohol to a white paper towel or a cotton ball. If the spot is deep in the carpet fibers, use a blotting motion until the spot is removed or no color is transferred to the cloth. If the spot is on the surface only, rub in one direction at a time. If the spot isn't gone, apply the detergent solution on page 151, blot, and continue as long as the spot is coming out. Rinse with plain water, blot, spray with water, apply a weighted pad, and allow to dry. If any stain remains, apply OxiClean, Resolve, or Capture according to the label directions.

PET URINE

If it's dry: Apply the detergent solution on page 151 and blot. Apply the vinegar solution on page 151 and blot. Apply the ammonia solution on page 151 and blot. Apply the detergent solution again and blot. Sponge with plain water and blot again.

If it's fresh: Blot, then apply the ammonia solution and blot again. Apply the detergent solution and blot. Sponge with plain water and blot again.

RED WINE

Neutralize by saturating the spot with the vinegar solution on page 151, and blot to remove excess moisture. Apply the detergent solution on page 151 and blot, repeating as long as the spot is coming out. Rinse with plain water, blot, spray with water, apply a weighted pad, and allow to dry. If any stain remains, apply OxiClean, Resolve, or Capture according to the label directions.

VOMIT

Remove any residue and blot the stain with cotton towels. Neutralize the area by spraying with the ammonia solution on page 151 and blot. Apply the detergent solution on page 151 and work it in with a blotting motion. Rinse with plain water, blot, spray with water, cover with a weighted pad, and allow to dry. If there's still some stain, lightly moisten with 3 percent hydrogen peroxide, cover with a weighted pad, and let stand for one hour.

TREATING THE STAINS

When you see the directive to "apply" a solution in the following instructions, you can do whatever makes the most sense given the size of the stain and the tools at your disposal. For a tiny spot you might just add a few drops of cleaning solution with an eyedropper, or dab it on with a cotton ball or the edge of a towel or sponge. For a larger stain, you could spritz the area using a spray bottle, which allows you to control pretty precisely how much solution you apply. You could also squeeze a sponge saturated with solution above the stain to sparingly dribble solution onto it. Whatever method you use, try never to *soak* the carpet.

WATER-BASED STAINS

CAUSED BY

Alcohol	Felt-tip Marker	Graphite	Soil spots
Baby formula	Food stains (general)	Ice cream	Syrup
Blood		Jelly	Tomato juice
Candy	Fruit juice	Ketchup	Water colors
Chocolate milk	Fruit punch	Latex paint	Watermelon
Clay	Furniture polish	Liquor	Whiskey
Cologne	Grape juice	Milk	White wine
Cranberry juice		Soft drinks	

TREATMENT

STEP 1

✳ Use a spoon or a dull knife to remove solid materials.

✳ For large stains, work from the outside of the stain to the center to prevent spreading.

✳ Blot up liquid spills with a clean white cotton towel or a white paper towel.

✳ Mix a solution of $1/4$ teaspoon clear hand-dishwashing detergent with 1 cup water. Stir gently.

STRATEGIC **MAN**EUVER
The Spot That Won't Die

Even after proper cleaning, spots in a carpet may slowly reappear over time. This phenomenon is called "wicking," and it happens most often when a large amount of liquid has been spilled. Cleaning only removes the stain from the surface—the carpet fibers—but the liquid and stain can get into the carpet's backing and padding, too. Through capillary action, the stain can work its way back up through the carpet fibers and resurface.

The good news is that these stains can usually be removed by repeating the cleaning steps you followed the first time you treated them. When you're finished, place white paper towels or white cotton towels weighted down with a heavy object over the area while the carpet dries.

* Apply the detergent solution directly to a white cotton cloth. Dampen the carpet fibers in the stained area with the cloth. Avoid saturating the carpet.
* Wipe gently. Turn the cloth frequently. Never rub, scrub, or use a brush—this may damage carpet fibers.
* If necessary, use your fingertips to work the solution to the base of the stain.
* Wet the stained carpet fibers with clear, lukewarm water to rinse.
* Cover the spot with an absorbent white cotton towel or a white paper towel and apply pressure to blot.
* Repeat the rinsing and blotting procedures until you are sure all traces of the detergent have been removed.
* If the stain is gone, place several absorbent white cotton towels or white paper towels over the area cleaned, and weigh the towels down with a heavy, color-fast object like a weighted plastic wastebasket or a brick.

* Change the cotton towels or paper towels until the carpet dries.
* If the stain remains, go to step 2.

STEP 2

Do not do the following for coffee, tea, or urine stains.

* Mix 2 tablespoons nonbleaching, nonsudsing household ammonia with 1 cup lukewarm water.
* Apply the ammonia solution, rinse, and blot as outlined in step 1.
* Do not dry with paper towels. Proceed to step 3 to neutralize the ammonia solution.

STEP 3

* Mix 1 cup white vinegar with 2 cups water.
* Apply the vinegar solution, rinse, and blot as outlined in step 1.

GREASY, OIL-BASED STAINS

CAUSED BY

Butter	Furniture polish (oil-based)	Lipstick	Ointment
Chocolate		Margarine	Olive oil
Cooking oil	Gravy	Mascara	Peanut butter
Cosmetics	Grease	Mayonnaise	Rouge
Crayon	Hand cream	Nail polish	Salad dressing
Furniture dye	Ink	Oil	Spaghetti
		Oil paint	Varnish

TREATMENT

STEP I

* Use a spoon or a dull knife to remove solid materials.
* Apply isopropyl rubbing alcohol to a clean white cotton cloth, a white paper towel, or a cotton ball. Don't saturate the carpet. Blot until the spot is removed or no color is transferred to the cloth. If the spot isn't coming out, go to step 2.

HOME **MAN**AGEMENT TIP
Dents in the Carpet

Did you rearrange the furniture lately? Or just move it a little? If the room is carpeted, you most likely left noticeable dents wherever the furniture feet rested. There are two ways to eliminate them:

1. Put an ice cube into each indentation. After it has melted and the liquid has evaporated, the dent should be gone.

2. Hold a steam iron just above the indentation—don't touch the carpet. After steaming the dent out, fluff the carpet pile with your hand or a brush.

To minimize dents in the future, you can occasionally move the furniture a bit so that it's not always pressing on the same point and constantly stressing the same carpet fibers.

STEP 2

* For large stains, work from the outside of the stain to the center to prevent spreading.
* Blot up liquid spills with a clean white cotton towel or a white paper towel.
* Mix a solution of 1/4 teaspoon clear hand-dishwashing detergent with 1 cup water. Stir gently.
* Apply the detergent solution directly to a white cotton cloth. Dampen the carpet fibers in the stained area with the cloth. Avoid saturating the carpet.
* Wipe gently. Turn the cloth frequently. Never rub, scrub, or use a brush—this may damage carpet fibers.
* If necessary, use your fingertips to work the solution to the base of the stain.
* Wet the stained carpet fibers with clear, lukewarm water to rinse.

* Cover the spot with an absorbent white cotton towel or a white paper towel and apply pressure to blot.
* Repeat the rinsing and blotting procedures until you are sure all traces of the detergent have been removed.
* If the stain is gone, place several absorbent white cotton towels or white paper towels over the area cleaned, and weight the towels down with a heavy, color-fast object like a weighted plastic wastebasket or a brick.
* Change the cotton towels or paper towels until the carpet dries.
* If the stain remains, go to step 3.

STEP 3

Do not do the following for coffee, tea, or urine stains.

* Mix 2 tablespoons nonbleaching, nonsudsing household ammonia with 1 cup lukewarm water.
* Apply the ammonia solution, rinse, and blot as outlined in step 2.
* Do not dry with paper towels. Proceed to step 4 to neutralize the ammonia solution.

STEP 4

* Mix 1 cup white vinegar with 2 cups water.
* Apply the vinegar solution, rinse, and blot as outlined in step 2.

REMOVING GLUE, GUM, AND WAX

GLUE

The following applies only to white glues and school glues. For other types of glue, follow the directions on their labels or packaging.

* Mix 1 teaspoon neutral detergent (containing no bleaches or alkalies) with 1 cup lukewarm water, saturate a cotton ball or cloth to apply, and blot with a cotton cloth.
* Mix 1 tablespoon ammonia with $1/2$ cup water, apply, and blot.
* Apply plain water and blot.

GUM

* The best remedy: Apply an aerosol chewing-gum remover, available at janitorial-supply stores, that freezes the gum brittle

enough so you can break it apart with, say, the handle of a table knife, then use a dull knife blade to scrape at the rest.

* An alternative: Put some ice cubes into a plastic bag and place them on the gum. When it becomes brittle, remove as much as possible with a dull knife.
* Mix 1 teaspoon nonbleaching detergent with 1 cup lukewarm water, saturate a cotton ball or cloth to apply, and blot dry with a cotton cloth. Repeat as needed.

WAX

* Scrape up as much as possible with a dull knife.
* Place white paper towels or a white cotton cloth over the area.
* Press with an iron set on low.
* Move the towels as the wax melts and is lifted onto them.
* If the wax is a different color than the carpet, apply and blot a spot remover or a carpet cleaner with a cotton cloth after first reading the product's label directions and testing it in an inconspicuous area.

Concrete

The garage is a man's domain, and yours is probably wall-to-wall concrete. Your basement floor might be the same if your lower level is unfinished. Taking proper care of concrete isn't hard, and it will improve your floor's appearance and lengthen its life. Here are some concrete examples:

* Seal new concrete to make it less porous. Or clean your existing concrete well, then seal it. Sealant is available at hardware and home stores.
* Sweep concrete floors often, and scrub them about once a year with water and a heavy-duty brush to keep grease and grime under control.
* To remove light stains, first brush with a solution of 1 gallon warm water mixed with $1/8$ to $1/4$ cup laundry detergent soap and 1 cup white vinegar.
* To remove tough stains, mix some TSP (trisodium phosphate, available at hardware stores) in a bucket of water according to

the label directions, slowly pour some onto the area, let it work for a bit, then brush with a nylon- or steel-bristle brush.

* Oil or fuel leak leave a puddle? Handle it ASAP. Cover it first with sand or sawdust to absorb as much of the spill and its residue as possible. Sweep or scrape it up, scrub with a TSP solution, then rinse. If there's still a noticeable stain left (you'll never get all of it clean, but . . .) apply a paste made of baking soda and water (1 cup baking soda mixed with about $1/2$ cup water), let it work, scrub it down, scrape it up, and rinse. And get that leak fixed, or put down some cardboard under the drip!

* Clean up *all* spills and stains as soon as you can, before they soak in. Remember, concrete *is* porous.

12

GRIME WAVE
Laundry and Clothing Care

I t'll all come out in the wash" is a familiar saying. I think it means that things are beyond our control until the very end, and by then God will have sorted it all out. Sometimes the same is true of doing laundry.

Washing clothes can be simple, unless you're a man. There are easy ways to do it, but there are also pitfalls that can make your favorite shirt look as if it were tie-dyed by a dyslexic hippie. So here are the basics on washing, drying, and ironing, with a few simple tips on sewing and dry cleaning. And a list of treatments for the most common man-stains on clothing begins on page 174.

Fabric Fundamentals

CARE LABELS

Your decisions about doing laundry actually begin when you're purchasing your clothing. Everything in the store will have a care label sewn into it, because manufacturers are required by law to stitch one into all garments sold in North America (except for socks, but instructions will be on the package). A garment's label

Your Guide to Fabric Care Symbols

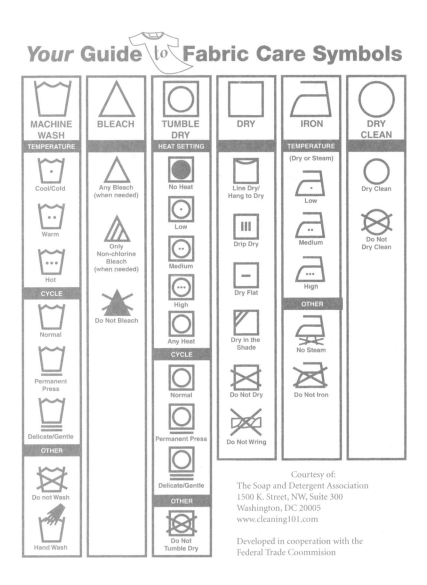

Courtesy of:
The Soap and Detergent Association
1500 K. Street, NW, Suite 300
Washington, DC 20005
www.cleaning101.com

Developed in cooperation with the
Federal Trade Coommision

You can find this chart on the website of the Soap and Detergent Association, 1500 K Street NW, Suite 300, Washington, DC 20005; www.cleaning101.com. It is reprinted here with permission.

provides you with your first clue as to how difficult or expensive it will be to keep a garment clean and presentable.

Care labels will tell you what the fabric is—cotton, wool, silk, linen, polyester, nylon, rayon, etc., or a blend of two or more fabrics, like "50% cotton/50% polyester"—and will include instructions for washing and drying. Most often the label will read something like "100% cotton, machine wash with like colors, use only non-chlorine bleach if needed, tumble dry, warm iron," or a variation on that theme.

For those who prefer not to read, the label will also include clothing care symbols that indicate how to wash, dry, and iron a garment, or whether to dry clean it. These symbols are not what you'd call intuitive. It can be difficult to figure out what some of them mean, so a chart appears on the opposite page.

Laundry Detergent

To get the desired results you should probably stick to the brand names you've heard of and pay a few pennies more. Laundry soaps are not all that expensive, anyway.

* Economy move: Go to a price club and get the biggest container of detergent you can find. If you use liquid, which I prefer, some of the largest quantities are in the neighborhood of 300 fluid ounces, which is nearly 2.5 gallons of the stuff. That's *at least* a year's supply for a single guy, and even this much will cost only $10 to $12 for a well-known brand like Tide, Wisk, or All. Containers bearing mass quantities like this are real hernia-poppers and unwieldy. So when you get home transfer a smaller amount of detergent into a more manageable jug or container and use it for your everyday laundry needs.

* Powdered detergent is a little less expensive per load. It probably does just as good a job as liquid, and which one you use is a matter of preference.

* The newer your washing machine, the less detergent you'll have to use to get clothing clean, because their agitating, clothes-cleaning action is more advanced and efficient. I don't believe you ever have to use as much as the detergent instructions call

for, but amounts will vary by the size of the load, how soiled the items are, and the "hardness" of your water. (See page 169 for the hard facts on hard water.)

Machine Washing

Regardless of the brand and the vintage of your machine, or even if you use a Laundromat, there are several tried-and-true rules:

READ THE CARE LABEL

Unless you're familiar with a piece of clothing, make sure you know how to wash it.

MANDATORY ADVICE
Save a Torrent of Trouble

Washing machine hoses can and do burst. According to State Farm Insurance, these failures cause $100 million in damage to homes in the United States and Canada each year, soaking carpeting, woodwork, furnishings, and more.

The hoses lead to your machine from a water pipe and valve hookup running along the wall. They look like very short black garden hoses. The shutoff valves on the pipes are probably the same as the ones on the garden-hose spigots outside your house.

Check them regularly. If they're more than four years old, replace them no matter what. Two good hoses cost about $20 or less at the hardware store. Look for bulging (spots where the hose sides may be weakening), as well as signs that the hoses may be getting dried out and brittle, which causes cracking and leaks. Ideally, turn off the valves whenever you're not doing laundry to relieve water pressure inside your hoses and minimize wear and weakening. And *definitely* turn off the valves when you go on vacation!

CHECK YOUR POCKETS

Chances are you won't be washing a winning lottery ticket, but currency, written notes, Kleenex, and keys are common items that get inadvertently laundered. Gum is big, too. And washing a pen could spell disaster for a whole load, especially whites.

SORT

Your clothing should be divided into loads consisting of "like" items according to these sorting guidelines:

COLOR. Separate whites, medium-colored clothing, and darks so that you will wash them separately. You don't want light clothing to pick up bleeding colors, or a white shirt to get dingy because you washed it with some dark pieces.

DEGREE OF DIRTINESS. Don't wash heavily soiled clothing with pieces that are only lightly soiled—the latter will suffer for it.

FABRIC. Although most of a man's wardrobe probably consists of clothing with tougher fabrications like cotton jeans and poly/cotton T-shirts, there are delicate items that should be washed in a separate load, possibly with the machine set to the gentle cycle. Loose-knit sweaters come to mind.

LINT POTENTIAL. Items that tend to throw off a lot of pesky lint include towels, terry robes, flannel blankets, and throw rugs. Excessive lint could cling to other clothing, and if there's a meaningful contrast (say, white lint on a black turtleneck), you'll be very angry.

DON'T OVERLOAD

If the washer is crammed with garments, the items won't circulate well. Clothing won't get as clean, and the larger items will tend to get tangled up.

DON'T WRAP SHEETS AROUND THE AGITATOR

The agitator is the "arm" in the middle of the wash tub that whooshes the water around during wash and rinse cycles. Sheets wrapped around them become tangled and twisted more easily, preventing their cleaning. Just place sheets loosely into the tub for best results.

WHEN IN DOUBT, USE COLD WATER

Most detergents will work just fine in cold water, and colors won't bleed and fade as much as they would in hot water. Hot water will also shrink things faster. But hot water can't be beaten for white sheets and pillowcases or light items that have been washed and dried many times or are preshrunk.

ZIP AND TIE

To prevent snagging, close zippers on clothing. To prevent tangling, tie things like the drawstrings on your sweatpants or belts attached to your bathrobe.

TURN CERTAIN ITEMS INSIDE-OUT BEFORE LAUNDERING

These include sweaters to prevent pilling, jeans to reduce fading, and T-shirts with "art" on them to protect the designs.

PRETREAT STAINS

The time to do this is just prior to laundering the stained item (see "Stain Removal Guidelines" on pages 178 to 180).

MAKE SMALL REPAIRS BEFORE WASHING

Mend small rips and tears—they're not going to get any smaller after you launder them. Reattach loose buttons, too (see page 187).

CLEAR THE LAUNDRY SINK

If your washer hose empties each load's water into an adjacent sink, make sure there's nothing in that sink (especially stray pieces of clothing) that could plug its drain and cause it to overflow. Your washer uses a surprisingly large amount of water—more than enough to overflow a sink if it can't drain—and if your basement carpet gets soaked, it'll cost you some major ching to resize or replace it. See "Save a Torrent of Trouble" on page 166 to find out how to prevent an even larger, costlier basement flood.

HOME **MAN**AGEMENT TIP
When Hard Is *Not* Good

If your soaps and shampoos don't lather well, if there's a white mineral buildup around your faucets, or if you notice a whitish residue on your clothing, you can probably assume that your home's water is "hard": It contains more minerals than it should. Hard water doesn't dissolve soaps and detergents as well as soft, and when the soap is less effective it's tougher to get things clean.

Your local water utility can tell you how hard your water is. If it exceeds roughly 100 milligrams of minerals per liter of water, you should probably get a water softener for the house. For this you'll have to use your plumber, or call a dealer in the "Water Softening & Conditioning" listings of the Yellow Pages.

Another remedy is to add a "detergent booster," which you'll find in your local supermarket's laundry section. But the more general water softener will improve your showers, baths, and dishwashing, too.

Laundry Additives

The general rule is to put additives (detergent, bleach, bluing, etc.) into your machine's washing tub first, then fill it with enough water to handle your load and allow adequate circulation during wash and rinse. Let the machine start, agitating the water a bit and mixing in the additives, then put in your clothes. And follow the label directions on all laundry additives.

FABRIC SOFTENERS

You can select either a liquid fabric softener that's added to the wash or rinse cycle or a transparent sheet that goes into the dryer with your load. Both types indeed make clothes softer, plus they reduce static and lint.

You can also buy detergents with fabric softener added, but these combinations aren't supposed to be very effective. The rap on liquid fabric softeners is that they add a filmy buildup on clothes if used too frequently. I prefer the dryer sheets for ease of use and the minimum storage space they require.

DETERGENT BOOSTER

Gotta use it when you have hard water that is overloaded with calcium, magnesium, and other minerals that make your detergent less effective. (See page 169 to determine whether you have hard water or not.)

BLEACH

If you've ever splashed chlorine bleach onto a dark piece of clothing, you know what it does: whitens the hell out of it. But under controlled laundry situations, bleach brightens fabrics by turning soil colorless and making it easier for detergents to remove it. It also sanitizes and deodorizes. There are two different types of bleach: chlorine and "oxygen."

CHLORINE BLEACH

Full-strength chlorine bleach leaves ugly white splotches on your good jeans. Here's how to use it properly:

* Dilute. Use according to the label directions, for white and color-fast fabrics only. Always read the label carefully.
* Add it to the washer tub as water is filling it, not after the clothes are in. Never pour bleach directly onto fabrics.
* Stick with a brand-name bleach. Generic bleaches vary in quality and may be stronger or weaker than you want.
* If you let an item soak in a water–chlorine bleach solution to remove a stain or general yellowing, don't let it soak too long (try a half hour at first) and don't be too heavy-handed with the bleach (start with 1/2 cup per gallon water). You can always do "longer" and "more" if the stain won't come out with one treatment. Bleach can weaken fabric fibers, possibly to the point where a garment literally falls apart.

OXYGEN BLEACH

Considered color-safe, it's milder than chlorine bleach and is made for keeping whites white and brightening colored fabrics. Still, add it to the wash after water is in the tub but before you put clothing in. Use it to launder colored items or whites for which chlorine bleach is not recommended. You can soak items in a water–oxygen bleach solution longer than in a water–chlorine bleach solution. Read the label for details.

OXICLEAN

As an all-around cleaner, this color-safe stain remover for clothes does a great job on most carpet stains, too, as well as grout, shower curtains, aquariums, siding and unfinished wood decks, lawn furniture, and more. As far as laundry goes, OxiClean is especially effective on organic stains like blood, protein, or food (coffee, milk, pizza sauce, etc.). It works well any way you apply it—presoak clothing in an OxiClean–water solution, or toss a scoop into the wash—but you can't use it with bleach.

BAKING SODA

Surprised? One of baking soda's multitude of attributes is that 1/2 cup added to your white loads is supposed to whiten and freshen laundry even more. I've tried it with laundry and have not really noticed a miraculous improvement in whiteness, brightness, or freshness of aroma, but it can't hurt.

STARCH AND BLUING

Starch makes garments, especially cottons, more supple and soil-resistant. Bluing is used to remove yellowing from white fabrics. Both are available at the supermarket.

Laundering Special Items

SILK

Dry-clean nicer silk items or hand-wash them in cold water with mild detergent. Rinse well, roll in a cotton towel to dry, and iron on "cool" while the garment is still damp.

LINEN

Dry-clean your finest linen garments or wash them in cold water on the gentle cycle. Dry on low, remove while still damp, and iron on the "wrong" side. Linen is made of flax fibers and is very sturdy, so you can use a hot iron for substantial garments but use a cooler one for lightweight linens.

POLYESTER

Admit it, you've got some in your wardrobe. Turn the garments inside out to avoid pilling, machine-wash in warm water, machine-dry on low, and iron on warm. Wear surreptitiously.

WOOL

Dry-clean woolens or hand-wash them in cold water, then dry flat on a towel (this is also called "blocking"). When the item (usually a sweater) is still damp, you can "shape" it with your hands. Don't put woolens into the dryer unless you want pilly, doll-sized clothes.

BLENDS

Clean fabrics made of a "blend" (for example, 65 percent cotton and 35 percent polyester) as if they were made of only the fiber that constitutes the highest percentage of the fabrication. But treat stains as you would for the most delicate fiber in the blend, regardless of its percentage of the fabrication.

DENIM JEANS

Launder separately in cold water for the first few washings—the color will tend to bleed. After that, turn them inside out when washing to minimize fading.

DOWN JACKETS, COMFORTERS, SLEEPING BAGS

Dry cleaning is a great option that eliminates guesswork and labor. Otherwise, read the care label: Washability depends on the fabric that the down is filling. In general, you should wash down items separately from nondown items. Make sure all loose seams and rips, even tiny ones, are repaired before washing. Machine-wash in cold water on the gentlest cycle and use a mild detergent. Tip: Toss a few tennis balls into the dryer with the down item to fluff it up while drying, and use the dryer's delicate setting.

DOWN AND POLYESTER PILLOWS

Read the label. Both down- and poly-filled pillows should be machine-washable. Wash two pillows at a time to balance the load for the spin cycle. Fill the machine tub with cold water and push the pillows down into the water until they're soaked and submerged, then wash for five to ten minutes on delicate cycle. Put the pillows through the rinse cycle several times.

Extra pillow pointers: If the pillows are very large, take them to the Laundromat and wash them in one of the big front-loading machines. When drying, add several tennis balls to fluff the filling. To freshen up pillows without laundering them, just put one or two in the dryer and run on "air only" for twenty minutes with a fabric softener sheet.

BLANKETS

Read the label regardless of the blanket's fabric. In general, machine-wash in cold water on the gentlest cycle and use a mild detergent. Machine-dry on "air only" or drape the damp blanket over a clothesline and let it air-dry.

Electric Dryer vs. Clothesline

Dryer wins.

Stains

Like carpet stains, garment stains should be dealt with as soon as possible after they happen. The longer the time span between mishap and treatment, the more the stain can "set," making it more difficult to remove. Instant treatment is often not possible, but men live for challenges, don't we? The next best thing is to treat the stain just before washing the garment.

Try to find out what caused the stain if you don't already know.

MANDATORY ADVICE
Treating the Most Common Man-Stains on Garments

The instructions below cover washable fabrics. If the garment label says "dry-clean only," believe it, and go to the cleaner's as soon as possible.

BEER

Try to treat the stain before it dries. Sponge the spot with a mild solution of $1/8$ cup white vinegar in 1 cup water, or use plain water if nothing else is available. Then launder according to the label directions.

KETCHUP, TOMATO SAUCE, BARBECUE SAUCE

Rinse in cold water and soak in a solution of $1/4$ cup laundry detergent to 1 gallon cool water. Apply a prewash product. Rinse. Launder if the stain is gone; use bleach if it's safe for the fabric. Otherwise, sponge the stain with a 50-50 solution of water and white vinegar, reapply the pretreat product, and launder.

COFFEE

Try not to let the stain dry. Rinse or sponge with cool water or soak for a half hour in a mild detergent-water solution. Launder.

COLA

Blot with water and a clean cotton cloth; sponge with warm water to get the sugar out. Launder as usual.

GRASS

Directly apply an enzyme detergent, or soak in water with an enzyme detergent added. If this doesn't remove the stain, sponge it with a solution of one part rubbing alcohol and two parts water. Launder in the hottest water that is safe for the fabric, and use a bleach (chlorine or all-fabric) that's also safe.

PIZZA GREASE, SALAD DRESSING, BUTTER

Pretreat light stains with a spray stain remover or a liquid laundry detergent before laundering with the hottest water safe for the fabric. For heavier stains, place an absorbent paper towel behind the stain, spray some dry spotter on the spot, then take a white cotton handkerchief and gently rub the spot. A dry spotter is a solvent-based spot remover that removes oily or greasy stains; it is sold in janitorial-supply stores and some home stores under the brand names Energine, Carbona, and K2r.

MUD

Let it dry, then scrape or brush off as much as you can. If the stain is not too bad, pretreat it with a liquid detergent before launder-ing. If it is heavy, presoak with a laundry detergent, preferably one containing enzymes. You may have to soak it overnight. Launder in the hottest water safe for the fabric, and use chlorine bleach, if possible, or all-fabric bleach.

MUSTARD

Treat with a prewash stain remover, then launder according to the garment's label directions. Use chlorine bleach, if possible, or all-fabric bleach.

PERSPIRATION

Treat with a prewash stain remover. Perspiration stains may respond best if the prewash treatment contains enzymes. You can also sponge ammonia onto a fresh stain or apply white vinegar to an older stain, and rinse in cool water. Launder in the hottest water that is safe for the fabric, and use chlorine bleach, if possi-ble, or all-fabric bleach.

PET URINE

So the dog was *really* glad to see you! Treat with a prewash spray, a detergent, or another product that contains enzymes. Launder the garment according to the label directions, using chlorine bleach, if possible, or all-fabric bleach.

FRENCH FRIES, POTATO CHIPS

Squirt some spray stain remover onto a white cotton cloth and gently rub the spot. For heavier stains, place an absorbent paper towel behind the spot and spray the spotter directly onto the stain. Continue until the stain is gone.

RED WINE

For fresh stains, cover with salt then rinse and soak in cool water. Treat with a prewash stain remover or a liquid laundry detergent, and launder with a bleach (chlorine or all-fabric) that's safe for the fabric. If the stain is dried on, try treating with an enzyme detergent, club soda, white vinegar, or ammonia, rising after each application.

VOMIT

Scrape or blot off all you can, then flush the spot with cool water. Soak in a solution of 1 teaspoon neutral detergent and 2 tablespoons ammonia in 1 quart water. Rinse with cool water. If there's still a stain, soak in an enzymatic detergent–water solution for a half hour to an hour, then launder. Use a bleach (chlorine or all-fabric) that's safe for the fabric.

When it's dry, a coffee stain looks a lot like a Pepsi stain. Learning what the stain is can clue you in to the most effective treatment.

Read the label on the garment to find out if it's washable or dry-clean only, and read the label on the stain-removal product to make sure it's okay for the fabric you're about to treat.

Don't rub. You may only succeed in damaging the clothing's fabric, spreading the stain, or driving it deeper into the garment.

Know when to cut and run . . . to the dry cleaner. When all else fails, or when you love a piece of clothing too much to risk ruining it, let a pro handle it.

There are many specific stain-treatment methods (see the chart on pages 178–180), but here are a few general ones to try before washing the item.

* First, test any stain-removal solution you intend to use on a hidden hem or flap to see how it affects the fabric and the color. If there's no damage or spotting, proceed.
* There are lots of prewash stain treatments on the shelves: sprays, sticks, and liquids. What usually works for me is applying Spray 'n Wash or Shout directly onto the stain, or soaking it in a water–OxiClean solution. Let any product work for a reasonable length of time, depending on the severity of the stain.
* Launder the stained item using the water temperatures suggested earlier, then check the stained area. If it's still there, repeat the same treatment or use a different prewash product, then rewash.
* *MANdatory: Do not put anything in the dryer or iron it if it's still stained.* The heat will "bake in" the spot and then it will be a *real* bugger to remove, if it will come out at all.

Always read the care labels on garments before you try any of the removal methods on the following pages. Each fabric has its own characteristics, as does each type of stain, which creates lots of combinations and different stain-removal rules, depending on what you're treating. These are general treatments only, for pre-treating garments before you launder them.

My advice, guys, is don't try to memorize every possible permutation. There are several books—*whole books*—that are dedicated to clothing stains, and *Clean Like a Man* will help you with the basics—including the most common man-stains (see pages 174–176). You can also call the 800 numbers listed on the labels of laundry detergents and stain-removal products if you want instant advice and personal attention (during business hours, at least), plus more details than the following chart provides.

If you are going to launder, refer to this chart. If the stain-removal methods described here or those you get from a product's help-line adviser aren't 100 percent effective, take your garment to the dry cleaner, show the stain, and let them know what methods you've tried.

Stain Removal Guidelines

TYPE OF STAIN	PREWASH TREATMENT
Ballpoint ink	Put the stain facedown on a paper towel, blot with a cotton ball or a cotton cloth soaked with rubbing alcohol, and repeat if needed. Then rinse and launder. *Or,* hold the stain against a towel and spray closely from behind with aerosol hair spray. The ink should transfer to the towel.
Beverages	Soak in cold or cool water. Rewash with a stain remover. Launder using chlorine bleach (if safe for the fabric) or all-fabric bleach.
Blood	Immediately rinse with cold water, apply a detergent containing enzymes, let it work, then launder. For dried stains, soak in warm water with a product containing enzymes. Launder.
Candle wax	Put the garment in the freezer or hold an ice cube against the wax to harden it, then scrape off as much as possible with the dull side of a knife. Place the stain between two cotton towels or sheets of absorbent paper and press with a warm iron, changing the paper until the wax is absorbed. If any staining remains, take the garment to the dry cleaners.
Chocolate	Rinse with cool water, then soak or prewash in an enzyme–warm water solution for a half hour or treat with a prewash stain remover. Launder.
Coffee	Sponge the stain with cool water, then soak in a mild detergent-water solution for a half hour if it's safe for the fabric. Launder.
Collar, cuff soil	Prewash or soak with a stain remover, a liquid laundry detergent, or a paste of granular detergent and water. Launder.

TYPE OF STAIN	PREWASH TREATMENT
Cosmetics	Prewash with a stain remover, a liquid laundry detergent, or a paste of granular detergent and water. *Or* rub with a bar of soap. Launder using a detergent with enzymes.
Dairy products	Soak in a product containing enzymes for at least 30 minutes (hours for older stains). Launder.
Deodorants and antiperspirants	Pretreat with a liquid laundry detergent. Launder. For heavy stains, pretreat with a prewash stain remover. Allow to stand for 5 to 10 minutes. Launder using an oxygen bleach.
Egg	Rinse in cold water, then soak in a product containing enzymes. Launder.
Fruit juice	Rinse with or soak in cool water ASAP. If safe, launder using a little chlorine bleach.
Grass	Treat the area by directly applying a detergent with enzymes, or soak in water containing a detergent with enzymes. If stains persist, sponge with solution of one part rubbing alcohol and two parts water. Then launder using chlorine bleach (if safe for the fabric) or oxygen bleach.
Grease Spots, oil	Pretreat with a prewash stain remover or a liquid laundry detergent. Then launder using the hottest water safe for the fabric.
Lemon, lime, vinegar	Rinse immediately with cool water.
Lipstick	First, gloat. Then place the stain facedown on paper towels and apply a prewash treatment. Replace the towels as they absorb the stain. Rinse, apply a detergent directly to any remaining stain, and launder. On pure linen, rub with a little salad oil to dissolve the lipstick, rinse, apply prewash or detergent, then launder to remove the oil.

TYPE OF STAIN	PREWASH TREATMENT
Meat juice	Rinse with cool, never hot, water.
Mildew	Badly mildewed fabrics may be beyond repair. Launder using chlorine bleach (if safe for the fabric). *Or,* soak in oxygen bleach and hot water, then launder.
Paint (latex)	While the stain is still fresh, blot up any residue and then rinse in warm water. Apply a detergent directly to the stain, then launder.
Perspiration	Use a prewash stain remover or rub with a bar of soap. If the color of the fabric has changed, apply ammonia to fresh stains or white vinegar to old stains, and rinse in cool water. Launder using the hottest water safe for the fabric.
Red wine	Quickest fix is to cover the stain with salt if it is fresh, then rinse with cool water. If the stain has dried, try saturating with club soda, then white vinegar or ammonia, rinsing after each application. You can also apply a prewash stain remover or a liquid laundry detergent and leave for 15 minutes. Always test for colorfastness first. Rinse and launder.
Scorch mark	Follow the treatment for mildew. But this stain may be permanent because the fabric is damaged, not just stained.
Tar	Scrape any residue from the fabric. Place the stain facedown on paper towels. Sponge with cleaning fluid. Replace the towels frequently. Launder in the hottest water safe for the fabric.
Tomato sauce or juice	Rinse with cool water, soak in a prewash stain remover, and launder.
White wine	Apply club soda, let it work, then launder.

Information in the chart comes from various sources, primarily the Ulster Linen Company, Inc., 383 Moffit Boulevard, Islip, NY 11751; 212-684-5534; www.pagelinx.com/ulsterlinen/removal.htm.

Miscellaneous Tips for Clothing Care and Laundry

MINIMIZE WRINKLES

Cut your ironing time by removing items from the dryer and placing them on hangers or folding them as soon as they're dry. This is especially good advice for shirts. If you forgot to get a load out of the dryer and the garments are wrinkled, add a dampened towel to the load and run the dryer on "warm."

REDUCE PILLING ON SWEATERS

Use fabric softener—either a liquid one in the washer or a fabric softener sheet in the dryer. And use a detergent that contains enzymes, which can help dissolve minor pilling on cotton fabrics.

LESSEN LINT

Keep your dryer's lint screen clear. Get into the habit of removing lint buildup before every drying cycle. And don't wash lint-producing garments like sweaters and towels in the same load with fabrics that attract lint, such as corduroy and synthetic fabrics. Also, an overloaded washer prevents loosened lint from floating free and being drained out during the rinse cycle.

AVOID SHRINKAGE

Use cold water to wash clothing, and run the dryer on "cool." Reduce drying time and remove garments from the dryer while they're still damp. Then either hang them up to dry, or smooth them out and place them on a towel on a table or counter, or on your bed, draped over the edge.

KEEP SOCKS MATCHED UP

If you actually have trouble with this, just safety-pin each pair together when you wash and dry them.

UNSTICK BALKY ZIPPERS

Apply a little soap to the zipper's teeth, run a pencil lead up and down the length of the zipper, or rub candle paraffin onto it to smooth out the run.

RETHREAD A DRAWSTRING

Pierce the end of the string with a large safety pin and work it through the channel. It's often not easy. And for some reason girlfriends and wives are really good at this.

KEEP JEANS FROM FADING

I like faded jeans. But if *you* don't: Turn your jeans inside out before washing, wash them in cold water on a gentle cycle, and dry them on the lowest heat. If you hang them on a clothesline to dry, keep them out of the sun.

MAKE A QUICK "CLOTHESLINE"

Use a spring-loaded shower rod to fit between two walls in the laundry room—it's ideal for hangers.

SPEED DRYING

Toss a dry bath towel into the dryer with a load of damp clothes. They'll dry faster.

The Laundromat

We can't all own washing machines. If you don't, your laundry options include a professional dry-cleaning establishment that also does washing. Then there's the less expensive alternative, that American-as-hotdogs institution, the Laundromat. Here's how to enhance your experience there:

* Sort your loads at home using the parameters listed under "Machine Washing" on page 166.
* Take plenty of coins, hangers for shirts, and a small sewing kit to repair little rips and loose buttons you notice as you're sorting and while other loads are being washed.
* Take along a small container of detergent and your desired additives—stain pretreatment, spot remover, fabric softener, etc.—rather than purchasing them at the Laundromat, which is much more expensive.
* Load all your laundry accessories into an extra box, a grocery bag, or an old gym bag rather than carry them loose.

* Check the machines before using them to make sure nobody left behind a garment that could bleed color or create lint, a pen, or another stain-producing item.
* Do relatively light loads. Even though you think you're saving money by jamming more wash into each load, your clothes won't circulate well, so stains and dirt may not be completely removed.
* When drying clothes, dry lightweight items (shirts, sheets, pillowcases, etc.) together and put heavier ones (jeans, towels, sweatshirts, etc.) into their own dryer. This way, all the items in each separate load will get done at about the same time, and you'll save money on extra drying.
* Hang shirts the *instant* they come out of the dryer to reduce wrinkles and minimize the need for ironing.
* You may take your wash to the Laundromat in a bag or a pillowcase, but it's nice to have a couple of boxes or baskets in which you can place folded items and keep them neat when you're taking them back home.
* Laundromats are great places to meet women. Give it a try!

Ironing

The first and most manly tip on ironing is to avoid it as much as possible. You can accomplish this in several ways:

* Remove clothes (especially shirts) from the dryer as soon as they're done tumbling and put them onto hangers. If garments are still damp, snap them a few times and then hang them on a line to dry, or place them on a towel on the edge of your bed.
* Some detergents and fabric softeners help to smooth out wrinkles during the laundering and drying process. The product's label will advertise this benefit.
* Hang wrinkled clothes in the bathroom while you take a nice, hot, *steamy* shower. This works especially well with knits like cotton sweaters and fairly well with worsted-wool garments.
* If you'll be wearing a shirt under a sweater, just iron the parts that will show: cuffs, collar, and, with a vest, sleeves.
* When packing your suitcase for a trip, roll up slacks to keep them relatively free of wrinkles. And when you hang shirts,

pants, and sport coats in a garment carrier, cover them with a dry cleaner's plastic bag to reduce wrinkling.

Sooner or later, though, you'll have to touch up your machine-washable clothes with an iron.

CHOOSING YOUR IRON

Irons can cost up to $150 for the really chichi Euro models. But like vacuum cleaners, steam irons have a point of diminishing returns, and it's measured by price versus features that a man really needs. It tops out around $40, but you can get a perfectly adequate steam iron for even less.

First, definitely get a steam iron, not a dry one. A steam model makes pressing (technically *lifting* the iron straight up and then lowering it back onto the fabric—literally "pressing" it) and ironing (*gliding* the hot iron over the garment) clothes much easier and more pleasant.

In this price range you can get desirable features: automatic shutoff, self-clean, anticalcium system to prevent mineral buildup in the vents, and a "burst of steam," which produces an extra blast of steam for especially tough wrinkles or hard-to-iron linens. The auto shutoff alone can be priceless, especially when you're halfway to your date's house and you suddenly don't recall whether or not you unplugged your iron.

CLEANING YOUR IRON

Yes, when you first get your iron you'll need to read the instruction manual to find out the right ways to clean and maintain it. Keep the soleplate clean to avoid sticky ironing or staining a garment with residue from spray starch or detergent that didn't completely rinse out of the fabric during laundering. If your iron has a nonstick soleplate, clean it frequently with a damp cloth. If the soleplate is metal, put a mild detergent-and-water solution onto a cotton cloth and wipe the surface.

If you notice a sticky brown residue on the soleplate, it's probably from spray starch. Clean it off with a paste of baking soda and water on a soft cotton cloth, then wipe that off with a damp cloth. Don't try to clean your iron's soleplate with an abrasive cleanser, steel wool, or anything that could scratch the surface—that would pretty much ruin its gliding capability.

IRONING TIPS

* Spray starch makes ironing easier by smoothing out the iron's "glide" over the fabric.
* Don't iron a garment if it's soiled or sweaty. The heat and steam will set stains.
* If your iron starts to stick, make dark fabric shiny, or leave any kind of residue behind on lighter fabrics, stop ironing and clean the soleplate according to the manufacturer's instructions, or use one of the methods described above.
* The dial on the iron will usually indicate what fabrics to iron at what temperatures.
* Don't iron over rubber or buttons (they could melt) or zippers (they could scratch your soleplate's nonstick surface).
* Most irons have a little groove just above the soleplate that allows you to iron "around" the buttons of a shirt.
* If you're ironing a fabric like lightweight linen or an expensive dress shirt, especially a white one, put a clean cloth or towel between its surface and the iron to avoid scorching.
* Keep your ironing board cover clean; steam from your iron may lift any stains and transfer them to an item you're ironing.
* Store your iron upright, not flat, so moisture doesn't drip out of the steam holes.

IRONING SHIRTS

Everyone has a favorite shirt-ironing technique. Some books recommend doing it in just the opposite order of the procedure I'm about to describe. The outcome is probably the same for both.

* Either start with a shirt that's still slightly damp from the dryer or use a steam iron.
* Lay the shirt on the ironing board so that the front-buttonhole side is facing up—usually the left-chest side of a man's shirt.
* Iron that surface from the tail (bottom) up to the collar.
* Then pull the shirt toward you and iron the next lengthwise sec-

tion of the shirt's body. It's as if you're "barrel rolling" the body of the shirt around the ironing board during this procedure.

* Iron only the body of the shirt during this procedure; bypass sleeves, cuffs, collar, and shoulder "yoke"—the piece of fabric between the collar and the top of the sleeve.

* When the body is finished, pull the shoulder yoke over the small point of the ironing board and iron each shoulder, including in back of the collar.

* Place a sleeve down flat and iron it so that the crease is created starting at the middle of the shoulder yoke all the way down to the cuff. This crease would face outward on the sleeves as you're wearing the shirt.

* Iron the cuffs.

* Place the collar, folded back near the neck seam (where it would naturally fold back), on the small end of the board. Press it flat and rotate until the entire collar is ironed.

* Wear with pride!

A female friend told me you should always press *multiple* shirts in a *single* session, as long as you have the iron fired up. This makes good sense. But as a man, I iron shirts one at a time on an as-needed basis. So I keep my ironing board in my bedroom near the clothes closet rather than in the laundry room.

IRONING PANTS

* Turn them inside out and iron the pockets.
* Turn them right side out and iron the hip area.
* Pick them up, align the creases, and place both legs sideways over the board.
* Lift the top leg and iron the inside of the bottom one, then flip the pants over and iron the inside of the other leg.
* Lay the legs lengthwise on the board and iron the outsides of each leg.

Mending

You'll throw away your Buttoneer—man's best friend for reattaching shirt buttons—when you learn how easy sewing can be. By "sewing" I mean reattaching buttons or quick-stitching a hem, because any needle-and-thread work beyond that is just not worth a guy's time. That's what tailors are for.

A MANLY SEWING KIT

You might want to keep a simple sewing kit in the laundry room or in your dressing room so that you can quickly take care of loose buttons, floppy cuffs, and other easy-to-fix clothing crises. Have one in your shaving kit for traveling. Assemble your own kit from the list of basics that follows, or purchase a prepackaged sewing kit at most drugstores. They're pretty inexpensive.

* A spool each of white thread, black thread, and "invisible" thread (like fishing monofilament line) that will match anything
* A packet of needles in a few different sizes
* An assortment of buttons—some white shirt buttons for sure
* A small pair of scissors or an X-Acto knife
* Optional: a needle threader, Velcro strips, iron-on patches

SEW A BUTTON

Once you get the hang of this skill, you'll be able to sew buttons onto shirts, slacks, shorts, and jackets—and probably figure out how to tighten up the flappy cuff on your pants if you need to. For more advanced sewing, which requires skills most men might never choose to develop, I recommend a tailor.

* Put a strand of thread into a needle so that at least 12 inches of thread is hanging on each side.
* Poke the needle through from underneath at the point where you want the button to be, and center the button on it.
* Place a toothpick or matchbook match between the button and the fabric so that you don't attach the button too tightly.
* Leave a 1- to 2-inch tail of thread on the underside of the fabric on your first pass. Then run the needle through each buttonhole and into the others from the top and the underside.
* Make a crisscross X pattern for the most secure fastening.
* Don't worry: Once you see what's going on, your common sense will kick in and you'll be able to figure it out.
* Take enough stitches so the button is securely sewn on, then take one last poke through to the underside of the fabric.

* Run the needle and thread through the knotty part of the button thread on the underside of the fabric to fasten it securely.

SEWING TIPS AND TRICKS

* To remove a button without accidentally cutting the fabric, slip a comb underneath the button so that the thread goes between the comb's teeth, then use a razor blade or an X-Acto knife to cut the thread.
* To secure and strengthen buttons, put a drop of clear nail polish (if you have it around) onto the top threads.
* Use a strand of dental floss for a quick fix without thread.
* Sew buttons onto heavy fabric with monofilament fishing line.
* To complete your mending task with fewer stitches, thread your needle with doubled thread.
* Cut the thread at an angle to make it easier to thread the needle. Don't bite thread in two.
* Try using duct tape or a safety pin to perform a quick fix on a loose trouser cuff or hem.

Dry Cleaning

You can't always blithely toss clothes into the washing machine. Care labels will tell you loud and clear which items are "Dry Clean Only." Dry cleaning is more expensive than laundering, but it has its advantages. It utilizes a chemical solvent called perchloroethylene with detergent to clean clothes without causing colors to run or fade or garments to shrink. Dry cleaning will also guarantee that your pleated pants always come back perfectly pressed, which is hard to accomplish by yourself.

MANLY ADVICE ON DRY CLEANING

* Don't dry-clean garments too frequently. The chemicals take a toll on fibers, especially if the item is delicate. You may want to order a "press only" if you're just dealing with wrinkled pants or a sport coat.
* Don't have a garment pressed if it's soiled. The pressing may turn invisible stains a light brown, and the stains you *can* see may well become "set for life."

* If you have a suit or outfit that consists of two matching pieces, clean them both at the same time. Even though fading is minimal with dry cleaning, slight color changes can occur.
* The sooner you treat a stain on a dry-clean-only fabric—or any fabric—the better. Let the dry cleaner know what the stain is and what methods or solutions you applied in trying to treat it yourself.
* Even if care labels say "machine washable," use your common sense. Dry-clean knit garments (like nice sweaters), huge items (like a king-size down comforter), and especially delicate fabrics.

IS YOUR DRY CLEANER GOOD ENOUGH?

Check out the finished product. Signs of a dry-cleaning hack include:

* Visible "dents" or ridges on the fabric from buttons that signal an amateur pressing job
* Missing buttons—a good cleaner would replace them
* Stains on light-colored fabric from sloppily applied dry-cleaning solvent
* Misaligned creases in pleated pants—lame workmanship
* Bunched shoulder padding in sport coats—no excuses
* Lots of turnover in the establishment's personnel, or a succession of young, disaffected space cadets working the front counter

You deserve better.

...... 13 ......

CAN'T YOU SMELL THAT SMELL?

How to Turn Odors into Aromas

Most women have an amazingly keen, almost canine sense of smell. Only their selective memory is stronger. With their nasal radar, females can smell out a pair of overused sneakers in seconds, whiff even slightly ripened garbage, and instantly zero in on shower mildew, a dank drain, or postpeak food in the fridge. Since men's olfactory sense is not as evolved, these odors may not bother a guy too much. But it's easy to eliminate them from your living space—and replace them with aromas so wonderful that even *you* will notice the difference.

Quick Fixes for Common Odors

BATHROOM

TUB, SHOWER, AND SINK DRAINS
They can clog with hair, toothpaste, and soap residue. Sand and other dirt particles also tend to settle into the lowest part of the drain's P-trap plumbing and catch even more crud that's prone to creating unpleasant aromas. So, every month or whenever it starts

HOME **MAN**AGEMENT TIP
Everyday Items with Great Odor-Neutralizing Power

THE BEST HOMEMADE SMELL STOPPERS	WHERE TO GET THEM	WHERE TO USE THEM
Baking soda	Supermarket laundry section	Refrigerator, garbage can, car interior, carpets, closets, all rooms
Cat litter	Supermarket or pet-supply store	Car interior, garbage cans, closets, all rooms
Vanilla extract	Supermarket spice section	Kitchen
Coffee grounds (fresh or used— both work fine)	Supermarket (cheap), Starbucks (expensive)	Refrigerator, freezer, closets, car
Fabric softener sheets	Supermarket laundry section	Clothes drawers
Activated charcoal	Pet store, drugstore	Refrigerator
Newspapers	The paperboy	Wood product interiors (drawers, chests, etc.)

to drain sluggishly, add $1/2$ cup baking soda, followed by $1/2$ cup white vinegar. It will fizz when it's working. Wait for a couple of minutes, then flush with a kettle of boiling water (or fill the sink with very hot water from the tap, then let her go).

Another solution: After every use, or fairly frequently, clean the sink and shower with a nice-smelling disinfectant like Pine-Sol or lemon-scented Lysol. And to *maintain* that fresh smell, pour just a little of that same cleaner into the drain and leave it there.

MILDEW IN THE SHOWER OR ON THE CURTAIN

Mildew may not smell bad to you right now, but it's probably plenty noticeable to a perky female nose. Sponge it off using a mild solution of 1 ounce (1/8 cup) bleach to 1/2 gallon water, or a similar ammonia-water solution. Use rubber gloves. And remember: Never mix any two cleaning solvents together! And don't splash bleach on your clothing.

KITCHEN

COOKING ODORS

* Open a window to air the place out—an obvious but frequently overlooked solution.
* Use the vent/blower that's above your range when preparing strong-smelling foods (fish, broccoli, cabbage, etc.).
* Spray an air freshener like Glade after cooking.

DISHWASHER

* Rinse used dishes well before putting them into the washer. Make sure most of the food residue is gone.
* Toss 1/4 cup baking soda into the bottom of the dishwasher between uses, especially if you often go for several days or more before running the appliance.

STRATEGIC MANEUVER
Women, Smells, and Sex Appeal

Females can become sexually aroused by their favorite scents. (Men are more visual creatures, which is why Hugh Hefner is rich.) So if you're entertaining a babe, keep your habitat smelling great. Or at the very least, smelling "neutral." You'll find some great tips later on in this chapter.

GARBAGE CONTAINER

* Put cat litter (about a 1-inch layer) on the bottom, underneath whatever kind of liner you're using. (You *should* be using some sort of liner bag in the garbage can.)
* Remove garbage often (plastic bag liners make this easy).
* When changing the bag, spritz the container's interior with Lysol.
* Spritz and clean the container occasionally with Lysol or with a mild solution of Pine-Sol and water.

GAS SMELL (NATURAL GAS)!

Don't fool around with this, wherever or whenever you smell it in your home. If it's a heavy smell, it may be a leaky gas line to your stove. Take these steps immediately:

* Extinguish any flames in or near the kitchen (on the stove burner, pilot light, etc.).
* Do not turn on a light or use the phone. Either one could create a spark.
* Open the windows and get out of the house.
* Call the gas company ASAP from a cell phone, a pay phone, or a neighbor's house.

If you detect just a slight gas smell, a burner may have been turned on without lighting, or (much less likely) your pilot light went out.

* Make sure all stove and oven knobs are turned off.
* Open the windows and air out the room completely.

• • • • • • • **Olfactory Fact**

A dog's sense of smell is over 100 times more powerful than a man's. That's why you can't sniff out high explosives or pheasants. But then, dogs can't spray Glade around the room, either.

HOME **MAN**AGEMENT TIP
Get Rid of the Smell's Source

Aerosol spray fragrances like Glade and carpet powders like Carpet Fresh are just fine for quick fixes, but they won't eliminate what's *causing* the odors. That's the important thing for you to do: Get rid of what it is that actually stinks.

If the kitchen garbage is getting gamy . . .

1. *Short-term solution*: Spray the area with an aerosol; toss some baking soda on top of the garbage.
2. *Better solution*: Put a 1-inch layer of cat litter on the bottom of the garbage container, under the bag. This can be a permanent layer if you use plastic or paper bags to line your trash can.
3. *Best solutions:* Take the garbage out frequently. Use a plastic liner bag in your wastebasket to make removing the garbage easier and keep the wastebasket itself cleaner. Clean the offensive-smelling container as needed. If it has residue on it, take it outside and rinse it off with the garden hose, or clean it in your laundry-room sink. If it just has an unpleasant aroma, spritz it with a scented disinfectant like Pine-Sol and sponge off. Or pour a capful of Pine-Sol into the plastic garbage bags to create a pleasant aroma *and* keep the dog out of the garbage.

✱ Relight the pilot light (instructions should be visible and readable when you lift the stovetop).

✱ Still an odor? Get out of Dodge and call the gas company from somewhere else.

REFRIGERATOR

FOOD TIPS

✱ Toss out any foods and beverages that are gamy, postpeak (seriously beyond the freshness date), or growing hair.

MANDATORY ADVICE
Baking Soda and Cat Litter Rule!

Both are absolute "must-haves" when it comes to absorbing odors. They're effective, inexpensive deodorizers and they have dehumidifying powers as well, which is just the ticket for closets. To deodorize most spaces (fridge, closets, laundry chute, drawers, garbage area, even your car): Put either baking soda or cat litter into any open container or container with openings. There's no need to get fancy because the container will usually be out of sight.

* I prefer to put the baking soda inside a clean plastic cottage cheese or deli container with large holes punched or drilled in the cover. A bowl or an opened baking soda box are fine, too.
* Fill a cotton sock or nylon stocking with cat litter and tie off the top. Hang it in all sorts of odd spaces (laundry chutes, closet hanger rods, coathooks, etc.) or just place wherever needed.

(I've never tried combining the two products, but the cumulative effect could be one of those multimillion-dollar ideas waiting to happen.)

* Keep all food in sealed bags, wrapped, or in covered containers.
* Line meat and veggie drawers with paper towels. This minimizes moisture and odors.

GENERAL TIPS

* Place a container filled with new or used coffee grounds or a small box of baking soda on the top shelf. Change it every month or two.
* Sponge down the inside walls and shelves with a mild cleaner or a water-vinegar solution every few months. (Well, okay: Make it twice a year if you think of it.)

✳ Keep the refrigerator's cooling coils dust-free so that they're working at peak efficiency. Brush the dust off them every few months (see page 57).

SINK DRAIN

✳ Add 1/2 cup baking soda followed by an optional 1/2 cup white vinegar, wait a few minutes, then run hot water to flush the drain.

✳ After that, and on an ongoing basis, pour a *little* Pine-Sol or lemon-scented Lysol into the drain. Either of these solutions can be diluted in water without diminishing their aromatic power much. A wonderfully clean fragrance will endure in the kitchen. This tip applies to bathroom and laundry-room drains, too.

GARBAGE DISPOSAL

✳ Follow the same procedure you used to deodorize the sink drain: baking soda, vinegar, hot water.

✳ To keep the blades clean, degreased, and odor-free, throw in a good number of ice cubes while running the disposal. Run plenty of cold water while you're doing this.

✳ Occasionally clean the underside of the rubber gasket that covers the disposal's drain hole with a baking soda paste used with one of your cleaning brushes or a Scotch-Brite sponge. This area is often overlooked, but grime and slime can really build up there.

✳ Each time you use the disposal, run cold water for thirty seconds after you turn it off to completely wash food residue down the drain. Optional: Put 1/4 cup baking soda or white vinegar into the disposal between uses.

WOOD CANISTERS, BOXES, DRAWERS

If they develop a musty odor, fill them with crumpled newspapers or coffee grounds to absorb the odor and seal. They should smell fresh after a few days.

FISH SMELL

If you just made fish for dinner and your hands smell like it, rub them with lemon juice or vinegar and then rinse with water. Several sources claim that mouthwash removes fish smells from skin.

If your cutting board also smells of fish, rinsing it with white vinegar removes the odor.

BEDROOM

BEDDING AND MATTRESS

Sprinkle a bit of baking soda or carpet freshener on top of the stripped mattress. Leave it all day or for several hours, then vacuum. Or sprinkle a small amount of baking soda or carpet freshener between the mattress and the box spring, and simply leave it for the long term.

CLOSETS

A container of baking soda, cat litter, or activated charcoal placed on a closet shelf will keep musty odors away and will help keep the air dry, too. Hang an old sweat sock or a nylon stocking filled with cat litter from one of the clothing bars. Wash or dry-clean any clothing that may be causing the odor.

DRESSER DRAWERS

Put a fabric-softener sheet into each drawer, and replace it as needed to keep the drawer smelling fresh. You can also use cat litter or baking soda in appropriate containers. And never store soiled or sweaty clothes in drawers. Launder them first.

CAR

GENERAL DEODORIZING

Put a small container of cat litter, baking soda, activated charcoal, or coffee grounds into the trunk or under one of the seats. Or hang one of those little cardboard pine-scented trees from your rearview mirror, along with your fuzzy dice.

ASHTRAY

Put cat litter or baking soda right into the ashtray. It helps to deodorize the whole interior. You can extinguish cigarettes in the ashtray and replace the cat litter or baking soda as needed. It really reduces the odors of stale smoke and butts in a vehicle.

HOME **MAN**AGEMENT TIP
Banishing Odor in Fabrics

Get rid of odors in fabrics (clothes, carpeting, upholstery, and drapes) as soon as you can. The longer you leave them untreated, the deeper the smells will penetrate the fabric and the tougher they'll be to eliminate. This applies to anything that you spill, sit on, or roll in.

To remove smoky odors in clothing, fill a bathtub with hot water, mix in 1 cup white vinegar, hang the smoky clothes over it, and keep the bathroom door closed overnight.

CAR CARPETS

Sprinkle baking soda or carpet freshener onto the carpet and leave it on for as long as you like (a minute, an hour, or overnight). Then vacuum it up. Or sprinkle deodorizing powder *under* the floor mats, where you can leave it indefinitely.

Odor Preventions and Cures

You can use the following tips to keep undesirable scents from establishing permanent residence in your home, clothes, car, and other belongings—or to get rid of them once they do.

BASEMENT MILDEW

* Use a dehumidifier with a hose attached to the unit's reservoir, constantly draining condensed water into one of your laundry-room drains. This keeps the air dry.
* Place multiple containers of baking soda and/or cat litter in several areas.
* If you have a chronically damp basement where mildew just keeps coming back, you may need professional help.

CARPET OR RUG

* Sprinkle baking soda or carpet freshener onto the carpet surface, leave for at least ten minutes or as long as you want, and vacuum.
* For strong odors (pet urine, spilled milk, etc.): Call a carpet-cleaning service.
* If a mildew smell is actually in the carpet, you may have to replace the carpet. (Ouch! Consult a professional carpet cleaner to make sure.)

CIGARETTE OR CIGAR SMOKE

IN A ROOM

* A scented aerosol (like Glade) or a carpet freshener is okay for quick fixes.
* Place vinegar or baking soda in containers around the room (preferably in inconspicuous places).
* Place cat litter in ashtrays and replace it every time you empty the butts (cat litter is very inexpensive).
* Open the windows and air out the room.

STRATEGIC **MAN**EUVER
Drive Women Crazy with Cologne on a Lightbulb!

This is a great guy trick that leverages women's fondness for nice smells:

* Put a few drops of cologne or perfume on a lightbulb (while the light is turned off).
* When you turn the light on, the heat from the bulb will activate the essence of whatever you placed on it and the scent will fill the room.
* The whole place will smell instantly sexy! The object of your affection will be at your mercy!

ON UPHOLSTERY AND CARPETS

* Try store-bought carpet freshener or a more industrial-strength type of dry carpet cleaner like Capture.
* Smoke tends to get deep into fabrics and carpet padding, and if you have a tough time getting rid of it, you may have to call a professional cleaner.

ON CLOTHING

* Spray clothing that smells of smoke with Febreze or another pre-wash treatment, and add some baking soda or OxiClean to the load. (Note: Don't use either of these powders if you're also using chlorine bleach.)
* Shortcut: Put clothing that smells of smoke into the dryer, set it on "cool" or "air dry," and add a fabric softener sheet.

LAUNDRY HAMPER

* Put a container of baking soda in the hamper, or just sprinkle it directly onto clothes (it washes out easily).
* Hang or place a sock filled with cat litter in the hamper.
* Do laundry more often, before it has a chance to get smelly.

SNEAKERS

Launder shoes in the washing machine occasionally:

* Remove all visible dirt from the shoes first, outside or in the laundry tub.
* Use the gentle cycle and a little more detergent than the directions call for.
* Air-dry only; don't place shoes in the dryer.
* Machine washing works even for leather athletic shoes if you don't do it too often.
* Take out the insoles if they're removable. Washing them alone is an option, because most of the sweat from your feet winds up on the insoles.
* Sprinkle foot powder or less expensive baking soda into your athletic shoes between wearings, either on top of or under the insoles.

STRATEGIC **MAN**EUVER
No-Fuss Aroma Producers

You can create a pleasantly aromatic atmosphere in many places that are prone to odors:

* Tuck a wrapped bar of soap in your suitcase or gym bag.
* Scatter scented candles around the house; vanilla is probably the most popular.
* Light incense to overpower any bad aromas you want to eliminate. It can get a little smoky, but it's extremely effective.
* Toss lemon or orange peels into the garbage disposal, or simmer them in a pan of water on the stove.
* Sprinkle a few drops of cologne on lightbulbs.
* Add a shot of Pine-Sol or another scented cleaning solution to sink, bathtub, and shower drains.
* Use air fresheners. Besides its famous aerosol spray, Glade has added a couple of products called Plug-Ins and Duet. Plug them into a wall outlet, and both constantly release your choice of aromas. Duet actually sprays its scent at preset times. Great for bathrooms!

ORGANIC MESSES

The faster you clean up and treat pet urine, vomit, or other organic stains on carpet or upholstery, the better off you'll be. You can refer to the specific treatments for specific stains discussed in Chapter 12 (see pages 174–176), but here are general directions that also minimize bad smells:

* Blot or scrape the main mess off and dispose of it.
* Treat the affected area with a stain remover if needed, then apply a bacteria-and-enzyme digester/deodorizer like OxiClean, which is powdered and mixes well with water.

* Follow the label directions. If you're using a liquid spot-and-odor remover, you'll be able to apply it either full strength or as a solution with water.
* Test a tiny bit of your cleaner on an inconspicuous area of the carpet.
* Pour it on, and let it work for a few minutes.
* Blot it up (don't rub) with clean white cotton rags. Blot from the outside of the stain in toward its center to avoid spreading the stain.
* Repeat several times depending on the severity of the stain and its odor.
* When the area dries, the spot and its odor should be gone.
* A product like Arm & Hammer Pet Fresh Carpet & Room Deodorizer is also worth a try.

PAINT SMELLS

LATEX PAINT

* Add a few drops of vanilla extract to the can of paint and mix it in thoroughly to neutralize the paint aroma. (Note: My pal Al, a professional painter, says he doesn't do this because he doesn't want to risk compromising the "integrity" of the paint. However, I have done it several times with no noticeable effect on the paint job.)

OIL-BASED PAINT

* Ventilate the area with open windows and a fan. Sorry, boys, that's the only solution with oil paints.

• • • • • • **14** • • • • • •

GOING PRO
Finding, Evaluating,
and Hiring a Cleaning Service

"A man has got to know his limitations."
—Clint Eastwood as Dirty Harry Callahan in *Magnum Force*

Do it yourself" is a thrifty approach to housekeeping that can save upward of several hundred dollars a month for penny-wise guys. And heaven knows that money can be put to good use toward greens fees, pay-per-view boxing matches, and better brands of beer. But sometimes the most courageous thing a man can do is admit that he is helpless against dirt and clutter, and trust in a power greater than himself: a housecleaner.

This is generally referred to as "going pro." The most common motive for shelling out your hard-earned cash for housecleaning is that you hate to clean the house yourself. Completely understandable. Some other very legitimate reasons include:

* You've scheduled a party at your place, or invited a date for a romantic dinner, and you have no time to clean.
* Your home is so shockingly untidy that you are completely K2'd—traumatized by the thought of cleaning it all up.
* You happen to come into some money.

Any of these situations is a good time to call in a SWAT team (Scrub, Wash, and Tidy). But how do you go about locating and selecting the best one? Some of it is common sense, but not nearly enough. So while men might instinctively know *when and why* to call in the cleanup cavalry, we still need advice on *how* to do it.

Cost

Housecleaners can be hired on a monthly basis, biweekly, or even weekly. The service will cost you anywhere from $12 to $30 or more an hour—which may seem like megabucks to many guys. You'll probably be closer to the higher price if you want someone good, or go with a cleaning service, or if you live in one of the larger, more expensive cities. On the other hand, you might luck out and find a semiretired neighbor who likes to clean houses for a little extra income, does a good job, and gives you a good price.

For a lot of guys, the money issue will be where the rubber meets the road. If you had a cleaning person in an average house or apartment once every two weeks, three to four hours per visit at only $15 per hour, we'd be talking $1,170 to $1,560 a year in cleaning expenses. Chances are, the cheapest cleaners or services will probably deliver inferior work. But for the more expensive professionals, you might be able to get a better price if you sign up for a "package plan": getting on a regular, long-term schedule. Housecleaning is a competitive business and you'll likely be able to cut some sort of deal. Ask about it; you have nothing to lose.

How to Get Started

I. ASSESS YOUR NEEDS

Decide what kind of assistance you really require:

* For light housekeeping (dusting, vacuuming, tidying up) an independent solo operator is probably okay as long as he or she is dependable and honest.
* For deep cleaning (heavy-duty tasks including windows, walls, upholstery, carpets, floors—the whole enchilada), a service that's actually listed in the Yellow Pages or recommended by someone you know and trust is a better choice.

STRATEGIC **MAN**EUVER
Cleaning Service vs. Freelance Housekeeper

Here are the advantages of each.

CLEANING SERVICE

* Services have more personnel, so they will be able to keep their cleaning appointment with you even if one of their regular crew is sick or on vacation.

* The company might send two or three workers in your team. Each may specialize in a certain type of cleaning and get those parts of the job done better than an individual who's a generalist.

* They will certainly take less time to do the same work as one person would, and therefore they will complete the job and be out of your house faster.

* Most services will do most everything in every room, even heavy-duty stuff like washing walls.

* Consider a service that specializes in the kind of cleaning you need most—carpets, upholstered furniture, windows—because they'll have the equipment most suited for the job, and do the fastest and best work.

FREELANCE HOUSEKEEPER

* Hiring an individual will probably cost less, even though you should ultimately judge the freelancer's value based on the quality of his or her work.

* He or she could be more flexible regarding scheduling.

* An independent operator could be willing to tackle chores a service might not want to do: your laundry, running errands, shopping, organizing, and more.

2. GET RECOMMENDATIONS

Female friends who've had lots of experience with housekeepers are your best resource for getting a list of prospective cleaners. Ideally, these women will also know how you live. Getting some names and numbers up front can save you quite a bit of search time, and it's probably the only way you'll find out about good freelance cleaners.

3. INTERVIEW THE FRONT RUNNERS

According to your tipsters, these are the cleaners who match up pretty well with your parameters of price, capabilities, a schedule that suits you, and a willingness to clean your place to your specifications. Contact them by phone and ask about the basics:

* What is their fee, and what does it cover? Make sure they do the things you want to have done.
* What is the minimum number of hours they will spend at your house, and what can you expect them to accomplish in that time?
* Who will step in if your cleaner is sick or on vacation? Remember, you'll be letting a stranger into your house, which may be a situation you'd rather avoid.
* What kind of training and experience have they had? There's no official apprenticeship system for housecleaners, but they should have worked with a person or a service who taught them proper techniques.
* What kind of cleaning chemicals will they be using? This is important if you're allergic or sensitive to certain chemicals. They should bring their own products and supplies, not use yours (unless, for example, you insist that they use a specific brand due to an allergy you have). A housecleaner without his or her own vacuum cleaner, however, isn't worth hiring.
* How long have they been in business? If they've been cleaning houses for years, they should be pretty good. If they're just starting, their hourly rates should be lower to reflect their inexperience.

If you get satisfactory answers to these questions, tell them your vision for the house—what you need them to do. If you're a typical guy, you'll probably say something like "Oh, just general cleaning," which essentially means that your entire domicile needs work. To help both you and your prospective housecleaner zero in on what you want, use the checklist on page 210. Some cleaners don't do certain housekeeping chores like washing windows, stripping the bed and laundering sheets and pillowcases, and cleaning the oven. Before you hire them, ask about *their* restrictions.

4. CHECK THE REFERENCES OF THE FINALISTS

You could feel ready to hire someone based solely on the phone interview, but fight off the urge. You might want to talk to the finalists face-to-face and really get a feel for what they're like. And you should *definitely* get references from each of your candidates and check them. *Absolutely* check them. You're giving strangers complete access to your house and all of your belongings. Chances are slim that they'd still be in business if they were crooks or fools. But you should take no chances.

So get two or three names and phone numbers from each candidate and talk with the references directly. (A "letter of recommendation" could have been written by the cleaners themselves.) If you're hiring an established service, call your local Better Business Bureau to find out if there have been any complaints against the company.

5. NEGOTIATE SCHEDULES AND RATES

You've probably already determined that the cleaner you decide to hire is within your price range and is willing to work on a schedule that's to your liking. But finalize everything to make sure. Don't be shy about dickering a little bit on price. You might ask about the possibility of a "volume discount" if you go with a one-year contract, or if you're willing to be flexible about accommodating *their* schedule.

6. GIVE THE GO-AHEAD

Make a list of what you want done on every visit—in order of priority—so they don't miss anything important or waste time on something that's already clean.

Also, make it clear *how* you want things done. Give explicit

STRATEGIC **MAN**EUVER
Housecleaning Checklist

Here's a top-line list of questions to help you get some idea of what type of housecleaning you'd like to have done. Check everything that applies, then use the list as a guideline when you're interviewing cleaners. This way you won't miss any important points, and you'll be sure they're willing to handle everything you want done.

What Cleaning Services Do You Need?

☐ Window washing
☐ Laundry
☐ Ironing
☐ Dishes
☐ Wipe down walls
☐ Wipe down woodwork
☐ Wipe blinds
☐ Organizing
☐ Carpet shampoo
☐ Vacuuming and dusting
☐ Clean bathroom surfaces
☐ Clean kitchen surfaces
☐ Damp-mop floors
☐ Strip and wax floors
☐ Change bedding
☐ Oven and stove cleaning

Other:

_____

_____

_____

Scope of Job

Number of bathrooms: _____

Number of bedrooms: _____

Number of living areas: _____

How Often Does Your Home Need to Be Cleaned?

☐ Daily
☐ Weekly
☐ Biweekly
☐ Monthly
☐ Bimonthly
☐ Seasonally
☐ Semiannually
☐ Annually

Whose Cleaning Supplies Will Be Used?

☐ Cleaning service's
☐ Homeowner's
☐ Both

Type of Residence?

☐ House
☐ Apartment
☐ Condominium
☐ Town house
☐ Duplex
☐ Other

Approximate square footage: _____

instructions: Launder dress shirts only in cold water; wash and change the bedding on every visit; make the bed in a special way; put fabric softener in the dryer with certain items; hang shirts and fold sweaters just so . . . whatever. If you're especially persnickety, you should actually *show* them how you like things done when they arrive for their first appointment. It's doubtful this will be an issue for most guys, however.

7. FOLLOW UP!

Inspect the job as soon as you can after it's completed, and definitely within twenty-four hours. If you have a beef, call the company right away, talk with them about it, and find out how and when they're going to handle it.

Other Considerations

BONDING AND INSURANCE

It's very important to make sure your cleaners are insured for liability—against breakage of any of your possessions and/or injury to yourself or to them—and bonded, which means any theft claims will be paid. They should show you written proof of both insurance and bonding. You should read it carefully to make sure all the policies are up to date, and you should also get a photocopy of their papers for your files.

The odds are in favor of nothing happening. But they might mistakenly spray Formula 409 on that Monet of yours, or they may suffer a freak accident themselves. Someone could bring a lawsuit and take *you* to the cleaners.

CLEANING PRODUCTS

Find out what products your cleaners use. Are you or anyone else living with you (girlfriend, wife, kids, gerbil) allergic to any of the chemicals they'll be spraying around?

TAX CONSIDERATIONS

This factor alone may convince you to use a service instead of an individual operator. If you pay an independent housecleaner or "maid" over $1,100 in a calendar year, the IRS says you also have to pick up his or her federal social security taxes and, possibly, state employment taxes. Go to www.taxsites.com/topics/nannytax to download the *Household Employer's Tax Guide*.

TIPPING

Give your cleaner(s) a little bonus when the holidays roll around. At least $20—anything less is rather laughable. Finding good housekeepers isn't easy. When you do, you'll want to keep them happy.

Carpet Cleaning

Carpet cleaners are also included in the "going pro" group. The phone book is full of them, and I highly recommend using professionals for this job. You could go with a sole proprietor—you know, one of those guys whose truck doubles as his office. He *might* do a good job . . . but it's a gamble. If you're not satisfied, chances are you're out of luck: He probably won't come back. You're usually better off selecting a company that can at least afford an ad in the Yellow Pages.

STRATEGIC **MAN**EUVER
Preclean to Stretch Your Investment

Tidy up before your cleaners arrive. It sounds weird, but it makes sense. You're paying them to clean, not to recycle, hang up your clothes, pick up newspapers and magazines, move dishes from the kitchen sink to the dishwasher, and so on. Performing these extra duties eats up their time and doesn't advance the ball on their main mission.

You can also buy or rent your own carpet-cleaning equipment to save a few bucks, but you could run into two problems: (1) It can be an ordeal to use the large, heavy machines from the rental stores, and you still won't get carpeted stairways very clean. (2) The smaller machines you can rent often don't have enough power to get soap residue completely out of the carpet, and this will turn your carpet into a virtual dirt magnet.

So for the big jobs you want done right, seek out a professional carpet cleaner and follow these guidelines:

* Make sure they are bonded and insured, just like the housecleaners. You should see a copy of their policy, and all the dates should be current. Ideally, get a photocopy for your records.
* Find out what kinds of chemicals they use, and whether the fumes might be a problem for you or anyone else in your household.
* Get a written estimate.
* Ask if there's an extra charge for moving furniture or anything else. Little surprise "extras" like this might not be included in the estimate.
* Ask for references and call them.
* Always follow up. As with your housecleaner, take a good close look when the work is finished, and let the company know right away if you're not happy with it.

Armed with all the knowledge in this chapter, you should have a successful hunt for housekeeping help.

15

ADVICE AT YOUR FINGERTIPS
Get Free Cleaning Tips by Phone

There's nothing like something for free. On the label of virtually every cleaning product there's a toll-free 800 number you can call during business hours—usually 9:00 A.M. to 5:00 P.M. eastern standard time—if you have any questions about using the product, getting the most out of it, or avoiding potential damage to items that are being cleaned. What's more, there are other advantages to calling these numbers:

✳ You can talk directly to a live person—a rare treat in this day and age! You may have to press a few phone buttons to zero in on the kind of advice you need, but in most cases you'll get through to a customer service representative pretty quickly if not right away.

✳ The people at the other end of the phone line know everything about their product and how to use it. They are specialists schooled in every aspect of the product you're holding in your hand.

✳ They can answer any question you have; if necessary, they'll put you on hold and find the answer in a minute or two by consulting a supervisor or one of the reference manuals they're certain to have handy.

✳ They will gladly extend their explanation beyond product information and talk about general techniques you can use to solve your cleaning problem. Most are happy to share a few tips and tricks that could make your task easier.

✳ Most of these representatives are women with nice voices. So be polite when you call—don't ruin it for the rest of us.

I don't know how many women take advantage of this secret treasure trove of housecleaning information, but I do know that not many men do. And that's a crying shame, because we're the very people who need it most.

The following list of website addresses will also give you some ready resources to turn to when you're in a jam. You can also visit my website, **www.cleanlikeaman.com,** for more tips, advice, and time-saving shortcuts.

Clorox
www.clorox.com

SC Johnson Clean House Journal
www.scj.brands.com

Orange Glo International
www.greatcleaners.com

Home and Garden Television
www.hgtv.com

iVillage
www.ivillage.com

Hints from Heloise
www.heloise.com

Arm & Hammer Baking Soda
www.armhammer.com

The Soap & Detergent
Association
www.cleaning101.com

How to Clean It
www.totallyclean.com

Tide Stain Detective
www.tide.com

Wear-Dated Carpet Stain Guide
www.fabriclink.com

Acknowledgments

Writing, like housekeeping, is usually a solitary experience. But I've learned that it takes an astounding number of people to bring a book to life, and I am extremely grateful to all the individuals whose personal support and professional talent helped take *Clean Like a Man* from concept to reality. At the top of this list are literary agent Marly Rusoff, whose publishing industry savvy is matched by her patience and generosity; editor Chris Pavone, whose keen eye and sense of style improved this book's content immensely; the talented team at Clarkson Potter, including Marysarah Quinn, Caitlin Daniels Israel, Mark McCauslin, Adina Steiman, and Linnea Knollmueller; marketing whiz-kid Kathy Mack; author Deborah Chase, for sharing so much of her time and expert advice; and ace graphic designer Jim Specht. I also wish to thank the many friends and associates who provided so much encouragement along the way: Bill Mockler, Mark Byer, *überdesigner* Stephan Faerber, Teresa Fogarty, Ann Hummel, Mary Premo, Steve Sherwood, Bob Horwitz, Susan Nowling, Coco McNulty, Jennifer Schmeling, Christine Dahl, Tara Collins, Monica Vierling, Joanne Ferris, Phil Premo, Joe Way, Jeff Medsen, Joe Zaspel, Joyce Lapinsky, Susan Hughes, and Donna Manion.

Bibliography

ARONSON, TARA. *Simplify Your Household*. Pleasantville, N.Y.: Reader's Digest Books, 1998.

ASLETT, DON. *500 Terrific Ideas for Cleaning Everything*. New York: Galahad Books, 1997.

BARRETT, PATTI, *Too Busy to Clean?* North Adams: Storey Publishing, 1994.

BEAUCHAMP, KATHY J. *Outwit Housework*. Campbell Press, 2000.

BERTHOLD-BOND, ANNIE. *Better Basics for the Home*. New York: Three Rivers Press, 1999.

BREDENBERG, JEFF. *Clean It Fast, Clean It Right*. Emmaus, Penn.: Rodale Press, 1998.

COBB, LINDA. *Talking Dirty with the Queen of Clean*. New York: Pocket Books, 2001.

CULP, STEPHANIE. *How to Get Organized When You Don't Have the Time*. Cincinnati: Writer's Digest Books, 1986.

HELOISE. *All-New Hints from Heloise*. New York: Perigee, 1989.

Household Hints & Handy Tips. Pleasantville, N.Y.: Reader's Digest Books, 1988.

Householder's Survival Manual. Pleasantville, N.Y.: Reader's Digest Books, 1999.

MASELLO, ROBERT. *The Things Your Father Never Taught You*. New York: Perigee, 1995.

MENDELSON, CHERYL. *Home Comforts*. New York: Scribner, 1999.

O'ROURKE, P. J. *The Bachelor Home Companion*. New York: Atlantic Monthly Press, 1987.

PINKAM, MARY ELLEN. *Mary Ellen's Complete Home Reference Book*. New York: Three Rivers Press, 1993.

PROULX, EARL. *Earl Proulx's Yankee Home Hints*. Dublin, N.H.: Yankee Publishing, 1993.

REES, CAROL. *Household Hints for Upstairs, Downstairs & All Around the House*. New York: Galahad Books, 1993.

SCHOFIELD, DENIECE. *Confessions of an Organized Homemaker*. Cincinnati: Betterway Publications, 1994.

SOBESKY, JANET. *Household Hints for Dummies*. Foster City, Cal.: IDG Books, 1999.

WRIGHT, SUSAN. *Clutter Control*. New York: Barnes & Noble Books, 1991.

Index